NO BULL

~~NOBLE~~ REVIEW

WORLD HISTORY

Standardized Test Prep for World History

A no-nonsense approach to prepare for class and the big exams

by Jeremy Klaff & Harry Klaff

About the Authors

Harry Klaff taught high school social studies in the New York City public schools system for 34 years. In 1993, he was the honored recipient of the John Bunzel Memorial Award as NYC's social studies teacher of the year. As a member of city-wide Justice Resource Center, he helped write numerous curricula in law-related education. For many years, he created the annual Model City Council project, in which students took over New York's City Hall for a day-long simulation exercise.

Jeremy Klaff has been teaching AP History classes for over a decade. His website, www.mrklaff. com has been utilized by teachers and students across the country for review materials as well as original social studies music. Jeremy has published Document Based Questions for Binghamton University's Women's History website, womhist.binghamton.edu. He has conducted staff developments for "Entertainment in Education" at both the high school and college level. In 2006, he was included in the Who's Who of American Teachers.

Table of Contents

The No Bull Approach

No Bull Review…*"because your review book shouldn't need a review book!"*

Go to page 149 and cut out my No Bull Review Sheets. Use them to help you study.

This review book is the most concise and to the point review available for World History and Geography. Our goal here is to give you everything you need to know for class and exams. Sometimes review books can be full of material that you just don't need to know. Or, they give explanations that are just as long as the ones found in the textbooks. The No Bull approach is to cut through the fat and give you what you want.

We, as authors of No Bull Review, are teachers. For years, we have been speaking to students to find out what you want in a review book. The answer? No Bull. You want the facts, clear and to the point. And …you want review questions. Lots of them.

At the end of this book you will find an intense review sheet. If you know all of the terms and definitions on the *No Bull Review Sheet,* you should find success.

The practice questions in this book are our own creation, and are based on the style of questions commonly used in the curriculum. They are questions that evaluate the most important themes of World History and Geography.

We hope you enjoy the No Bull approach. Thank you, and best of luck.

– No Bull Review

Religions of the World

Note: Throughout the book the abbreviation "c" (for circa) will be used to approximate certain dates.

Religions have been around since early human existence, and through history they have affected many political, economic, and social events. Today, some of the major ancient religions are still practiced by millions of people around the globe. One cannot understand world history without being familiar with the ideas and beliefs of the major religions.

HERE IS WHAT YOU NEED TO KNOW:
Definition: Animism and Shintoism

Animism is a belief that nature's animals, rocks, weather events, and even plants contain spirits that affect the physical world. Animism was popular in ancient Africa and Asia. Similarly, in Japan, an ancient religion still practiced is **Shintoism**, which means "the way of the gods." This religion worships *kami*, which means the spirits of nature. They also practice ancestral worship.

Definition: Monotheism vs. Polytheism

Monotheism is the belief in one God. Polytheism is the belief in multiple deities (gods).

Question: What are the main things to know about Hinduism?

Answer: **RICK**

R - *Reincarnation* - This is the belief that people, or souls, are born again and again until a state of enlightenment (moksha) is achieved.

I - *I*ndia - Typically, Hinduism's roots can be found in India near the ***Indus River Valley*** and ***Ganges River*** (explained later).

C - *Caste System* - This is a class system in India. Brahmins are the priests who make up the highest class. Then come warriors (Kshatriyas), merchants (Vaisyas), and laborers (Shudras). Untouchables are those outside of the caste who are the lowest on the social ladder. A caste can't be changed during the course of one's lifetime.

K - *Karma/Dharma* - Karma means the deeds that accumulate throughout one's life. If deeds are good, then one can rise in the caste system after reincarnation. If deeds are bad, then one's status will decrease in the next life. Dharma is a duty to honor the caste. This is done by fulfilling certain religious and societal obligations. Remember: Dharma and duty both start with a D.

Question: What other things should I know about Hinduism?

Answer:

1. Parts of the religion were brought to India by the **Aryans**, or Indo-European people who settled in the Indus River Valley as early as c1500 BCE.

2. The sacred texts are called the Vedas. The oldest one is the Rigveda.

3. Major settlements in India were along the Ganges and Yamuna rivers.

4. A long epic in Indian history is called the **Mahabharata**. It's a poem with over 100,000 verses.

5. The **Upanishads** were dialogues between teachers and students. They helped explain renunciation (getting rid) of materialism (possessions) and reaching a level of perfect understanding. Like other Hindu writings, these were written in Sanskrit.

6. The major gods to know are: Brahma the creator, Vishnu the protector, and Shiva the destroyer.

Question: What are the main things to know about Buddhism?

Answer: **BENN**

B - **B**uddha. Around 500 BCE, Siddhartha Gautama, a Hindu, was looking for *enlightenment*. He found it during a meditation session under a tree and became "The Enlightened One."

E - **E**ightfold Path. This is the fourth of the Four Noble Truths (explained below).

N - The Four **N**oble Truths. The crux of Buddhism is:

    1. That everything in life is suffering.

    2. This suffering is caused by selfish desires for fleeting pleasure.

    3. To end all suffering, one must stop desiring.

    4. To attain enlightenment, one must follow the Eightfold Path, which is a moral staircase of proper behavior.

N - **N**irvana. If one reaches the top of the moral staircase, they are released from selfishness and darkness.

Question: What other things should I know about Buddhism?

Answer:

1. It spread from India to other parts of Asia, specifically China.

2. It has similarities with Hinduism, but there is no caste system.

3. The Mahayana sect allows people to become Buddhas. The sect also allows all people, not just monks, to worship. This has opened up the religion to non-Buddhists. In *Zen Buddhism*, all people can attain self-realization and enlightenment through meditation.

4. The Theravada sect interprets the oldest teachings of Buddha.

5. Through trade, Buddhism spread to China, Korea, Japan, and Indonesia.

Definition: Jainism

Modern-day Jainism was founded by Mahavira around 550BCE. The religion believes that everything has a soul and can't be harmed. This goes for all living creatures, including insects. Jainists can not harm any form of life.

Definition: Confucianism

This is a Chinese philosophy based on the writings of Confucius c500 BCE. Confucius wrote the *Analects* and advocated harmony, good conduct, and enlightenment. He also believed in the order of mankind. He defined the major *Five Relationships* as:

    1. Ruler/Subject

    2. Father/Son

    3. Husband/Wife

    4. Older Brother/Younger Brother

    5. Friend/Friend

He also believed in *filial piety*, which means a respect for one's elders, especially parents.

Definition: Daoism/Taoism

Laozi wrote the *Tao Te Ching* (*Dao De Jing*) in the sixth century BCE. He encouraged people to follow "the way." This means to accept the forces of nature, such as the balances of *yin and yang*. These natural, yet opposite, forces complement one another. Yin is female and dark. Yang is masculine and light. The ability to live in harmony with nature is a central idea of Daoism.

Question: What are the Five Pillars of Islam?

Answer: **DRAFT**

D - **D**aily Prayer. One must face the holy city of Mecca and pray 5 times a day.

R - **R**amadan. This is a month where one must fast when the sun is up.

A - **A**lms. Giving charity to help the poor.

F - **F**aith in one God, Allah.

T - **T**ravel to the holy city of Mecca, Saudi Arabia. This pilgrimage is called the hajj. At some point in a Muslim's life, a trip to Mecca

Left to right: A Taoist Temple, a Buddhist Temple, and a Confucian Temple. All three beliefs still coexist in China today.

is necessary.

Question: What else should I know about Islam?

Answer: Remember, Islam is the religion. Those who partake in the religion are called Muslims. More specifically, Islam means to submit to the will of Allah. Muslim means one who has submitted.

1. ***Muhammad*** is the major historical figure to know regarding Islam. According to the religion, the angel ***Gabriel*** spoke to Muhammad on behalf of Allah. Muhammad then preached his monotheistic beliefs in Mecca. In 622 CE, Muhammad went on a 200 mile journey to Yathrib (later called Medina) in which he gained many followers. This is called the Hijra (Hegira).

3. The sacred text of Islam is the ***Qur'an*** (Koran).

4. ***Sharia*** is the religious law that governs the actions of a Muslim's life.

5. Muslim Empires spread Islam throughout the Middle East, western Asia, and southern Europe.

Question: What should I know about Judaism?

Answer:

1. Judaism is monotheistic, as Jews believe in one God.

2. The Torah is the sacred text. In the Torah, it is explained that Moses was handed the ***Ten Commandments*** from God. These contain the ten most important Jewish laws such as observing the Sabbath, and honoring one's parents. The Ten Commandments also outlawed adultery and murder.

3. The Kingdom of Israel was established c1000 BCE, and Jerusalem was its capital. Strong kings were David and Solomon. Solomon's Temple was destroyed by the Babylonians.

4. Jews were removed from the Roman Empire c135 CE. They then scattered throughout the world. This was known as the ***Diaspora***.

Question: What should I know about Christianity?

Answer:

1. Born between 6 to 4 BCE, Jesus Christ preached that people should love themselves, their neighbors, God, and even their enemies.

2. According to written accounts, or gospels, after the death (crucifixion) of Jesus, his body disappeared from his tomb and then reap-

7

peared to his followers. Many of the holy sites of Christianity are in Jerusalem in modern-day Israel. Jerusalem also has holy significance for Judaism and Islam.

3. The New Testament of the Bible was written by the disciples of Jesus known as *apostles*.

4. The head of the Roman Catholic Church is the *Pope*.

5. Christians were persecuted for hundreds of years in the Roman Empire. However, the Roman Emperor Constantine had visions of a Christian cross in the heavens. He put crosses on his soldiers' shields and won a battle. Persecution of Christians thus ended in 313 CE.

6. After the Fall of Rome, Christianity spread throughout Europe. In the much later Age of Imperialism, the religion gained strength in Asia and Africa. Note: people who spread religion are known as *missionaries*. Splits in Christianity (Eastern Orthodox and Protestantism) will be addressed in later chapters.

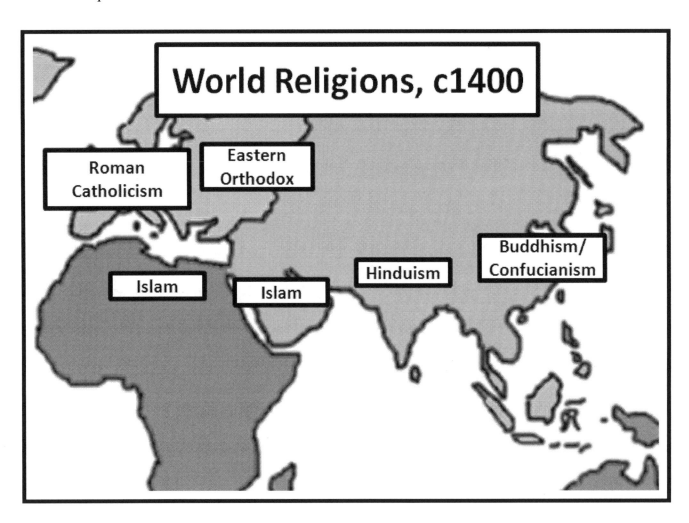

Review Questions

1. The pilgrimage to Mecca that all Muslims must take is called
   A) Sharia law
   B) the hajj
   C) the Qur'an
   D) Ramadan

2. Which of the following religions is most associated with worshipping spirits in nature?
   A) Animism
   B) Buddhism
   C) Hinduism
   D) Judaism

3. Which of the following explains a true relationship between karma and reincarnation?
   A) Good deeds will be rewarded in the next life with a favorable promotion in the caste system
   B) A person's good karma will decrease the amount of dharma needed to be conducted
   C) Favorable karma can change a person's caste before death
   D) Reincarnation is only rewarded to people in the highest castes

4. Jainism believes
   A) in a strict interpretation of the Analects
   B) that one should follow the Eightfold Path to nirvana
   C) religion should be spread by the sword
   D) everything has a soul and cannot be harmed

5. All of the following are true of Buddhism EXCEPT:
   A) Suffering is caused by selfish desires for pleasure
   B) Enlightenment must be achieved
   C) One cannot stop desiring no matter how hard they try
   D) There are Four Noble Truths

6. The Five Relationships and filial piety are most associated with
   A) Hinduism
   B) Christianity
   C) Confucianism
   D) Daoism

7. A similarity between Judaism and Christianity is that they both
   A) originated in India before coming to the Middle East
   B) renounce materialism and selfish desires
   C) enforce a strict interpretation of the New Testament
   D) maintain a belief in one God

8. Which of the following is associated with Islam?
   A) Tao Te Ching
   B) Analects
   C) Eightfold Path
   D) Qur'an

9. Today in China, which of the following would be practiced by the LEAST amount of people?

A) Confucianism
B) Daoism
C) Shintoism
D) Buddhism

10. A major difference between Hinduism and Buddhism is that

A) Hindus rely on rigid class distinctions within the caste system
B) only Buddhists believe in reincarnation
C) Buddhism began in Japan, whereas Hinduism began in China
D) Hinduism is monotheistic and Buddhism is polytheistic

Answers and Explanations

1. **B**. The hajj is a pilgrimage to the holy city of Mecca in Saudi Arabia. Performing the hajj is one of the Five Pillars of Islam every Muslim must honor.

2. **A**. Animism is a belief in honoring spirits and nature. Japanese Shintoism has similar beliefs in *kami*, or the spirits of nature.

3. **A**. If one has good karma, they will be rewarded with a higher status in the next life. Karma, reincarnation, and the caste system are all interrelated.

4. **D**. Jainists believe that every living creature, even insects, has a soul and cannot be harmed.

5. **C**. Buddha's teachings show that if one controls the source of their desires, they can reach a state of nirvana where no suffering occurs. This can only be done through years of discipline and introspective understanding.

6. **C**. The Five Relationships and filial piety (respect for elders) came from Confucius. The major themes of Confucian teachings can be found in the Analects.

7. **D**. Judaism and Christianity are both monotheistic religions. This means they believe in one God. Both religions have roots in the Middle East near the Holy City of Jerusalem.

8. **D**. The Qur'an (Koran) is the holy scripture of Islam.

9. **C**. Though there are Shintos in China, the other three beliefs are practiced to a greater extent. Shintoism is mostly associated with Japan.

10. **A**. Hinduism involves the caste system. Buddha disagreed with the caste system and did not incorporate it into his teachings.

Early Civilizations, Mesopotamia, and Egypt

The earliest civilizations began to develop after c10000 BCE. As humans learned to domesticate animals and harvest crops, they were able to enjoy new settled lifestyles. Major civilizations developed near sources of water such as rivers. From the *cradle of civilization* of Mesopotamia, advanced systems of writing, trade, law, and religious practice began to emerge. In nearby Egypt, incredible architecture was constructed with similar advancements in writing and worship. Eventually new civilizations, looking to amass great Empires throughout the region, waged war.

HERE IS WHAT YOU NEED TO KNOW:

• EARLY CIVILIZATIONS
Question: What do I need to know about the history at the beginning of my textbook?

Answer:

1. In 1978 an archaeologist and anthropologist named Mary Leakey found the oldest known prehistoric footprints in Tanzania, Africa. This was a hominid, or human-like creature that could walk upright. Leakey was able to examine early society by excavating artifacts, thus making her an *archaeologist*. She was also an *anthropologist* who studied culture and how people lived.

2. Early people were *nomadic*, meaning they consisted of wandering tribes. Specifically in the Middle East the term *Bedouin* is used to describe early desert-dwellers.

3. Many people were *hunters and gatherers*. Men typically hunted while women gathered berries, roots, and other plants.

4. *Slash-and-burn farming* meant that people cleared land for farms by burning trees. The ashes were then used as fertilizer. These same people *domesticated* many animals, or learned to train them into creatures that could help with the farming process. Such techniques would be a part of the Neolithic Revolution (explained next).

Definition: Neolithic Revolution

By 10000 BCE, early humans learned that seeds could germinate into crops. The Neolithic Revolution involved just that, and the results were greater harvests, permanent settlements, and a decrease in nomadic lifestyle. Many were *subsistence farmers* who grew just enough to feed their families.

Thus, in the Neolithic Revolution, hunting and gathering gave way to taming animals and harvesting crops. People could now stay in one place. This led to the rise of *civilizations*. Civilizations can be classified as a settled population with a government, local economy, and cultural and scientific advancements.

• MESOPOTAMIA
Definition: Fertile Crescent of Mesopotamia

Mesopotamia, *the cradle of civilization*, was situated between the Tigris and Euphrates Rivers in modern-day Iraq. *People settled near rivers for farming, water, and trade*. By 2000 BCE there was a thriving culture there, as complex ancient cities developed in Sumer, Canaan (Israel, or Palestine), and Babylon. Because of its shape and abundance of farmable soil, the area was nicknamed the "Fertile Crescent" by historians.

Definition: Cultural Diffusion

Probably the most important term of global studies, this means the exchange of ideas between cultures. This happened in Mesopotamia, and everywhere else in the world. Religion, technology, ideas, literature, government...you name it, it's been exchanged. You can find a list of major examples of cultural diffusion in the *No Bull Review Sheet*.

Question: What were the strongest civilizations in Mesopotamia?

Answer:

1. Sumer - Sumer was settled as early as 3500 BCE. People began to use bronze rather than stone in their weapons. This meant the ***Bronze Age*** had arrived. In addition, the Sumerians had an elaborate system of writing called ***cuneiform***, which was recorded on clay tablets.

Within Sumer was the city of Ur. They had pyramids called ***ziggurats*** which were used for religious worship.

2. Babylon - The Babylonians had a king named ***Hammurabi*** who enforced a code of law. Around 1750 BCE, ***Hammurabi's Code*** applied to everyone. However, sometimes it did so unfairly. The poor were treated harsher, and women had a lower status than men. Famously his code had laws that proclaimed justice to be "an eye for an eye."

3. Canaan (Israel or Palestine) - Under Kings Saul, David, and Solomon, the Hebrews established a strong Empire. Around 950 BCE, King Solomon's great Temple was home to the Ark of the Covenant which contained the Ten Commandments. The Kingdom was overrun by the Assyrian Empire, and eventually taken over by the Babylonian King ***Nebuchadnezzar***. The Temple was destroyed, and Nebuchadnezzar put the Jews into captivity c550 BCE.

4. Assyrians - This was a military Empire known for burning cities and slaughtering people. By 700 BCE, they had defeated nearly all of the Empires in Mesopotamia.

Question: What other Empires in the area should I know?

Answer:

1. Persians - In 550 BCE, ***Cyrus*** became King and the Persian Empire reached as far as India. Cyrus was tolerant of Jews, and allowed them to resettle in Jerusalem. Under ***King Darius*** the Empire spread further into western Asia. The Persians never took over Greece (explained later).

2. Hittites, c1400 BCE - These were Indo-European settlers in Anatolia (Asia Minor/Turkey). Their use of iron weapons helped them expand their Empire.

3. Phoenicians, 1500-300 BCE - They were maritime explorers who settled many cities around the Mediterranean Sea. Phoenicians are important to know because the Latin alphabet derived from them. Their writing system spread to cultures of the Mediterranean Sea, such as Greece.

Definition: Zoroastrianism

One of the oldest religions dating back to c500 BCE, Zoroastrianism is still followed today by a small number of participants.

It is based on the teachings of Zoroaster, a prophet in Persia. The religion teaches that the forces of good and evil battle for control of the soul. It is up to a person to fend off the urges of evil. After death, one's deeds are judged. Actions on Earth determine if one is permitted to have a blissful afterlife.

• EGYPT

Question: What is the importance of the Nile River?

Answer: The Nile is the longest river in the world (though some consider the Amazon in South America to be longer). Every year the Nile floods and leaves behind fertile soil. This natural event led to the rise of civilization in the *Nile Delta*. **Irrigation**, or the transportation and application of water to places far from the source, was accomplished to bring water away from the Nile. As in Mesopotamia, people in Egypt settled by the Nile for

Today, the most recognizable remains of Egyptian civilization are the pyramids and the Sphinx

agriculture, water, and trade.

Definition: Lower and Upper Egypt

Lower Egypt means the area that was in northern Egypt, closer to modern-day Cairo and the Mediterranean Sea. Upper Egypt was further south and closer to the city of Thebes. Around 3000 BCE, King Menes unified the crowns of each of these two kingdoms. This was the first of 31 Egyptian dynasties (chain of family-rule).

Definition: Pharaoh/Theocracy

Egyptian kings were known as pharaohs. The Egyptians believed the pharaohs were put in power by the gods, and ruled on their behalf. This idea is called a ***theocracy***.

Because the pharaoh had religious significance, their burials were of utmost importance. Egyptians used the process of ***mummification*** to dry out the body, and preserve it for eternity. Pharaoh tombs were buried all over Egypt. Notably, ***pyramids*** were built to house some of the mummies. The most famous pyramids are the three massive ones that dot the Giza Plateau outside of Cairo.

Definition: Hieroglyphics/Papyrus

Egyptians made use of a writing system known

as hieroglyphics. They used pictures and symbols to create a written record. The hieroglyphics were preserved on stone and parchment made from the *papyrus* plant.

One of the most famous historical records is the Egyptian Book of the Dead. The book details the judgment of the deceased and their hopeful journey to the afterlife. In the quest, the deceased person meets Osiris, a central figure of Egyptian religion. Another major Egyptian deity to know is Ra, the sun god.

Question: What Egyptian Kingdoms should I know?

Answer: The 31 Egyptian dynasties are divided into several kingdoms. Though it is not imperative to know all of them, here are a few of the kingdoms from c2600BCE-1000BCE. Subsequent kingdoms existed until the fourth century BCE.

The Old Kingdom was strong, but diminished in power. After a weak First Intermediate Kingdom, pharaohs grew stronger in the Middle Kingdom. Invaders known as the Hyksos took over Egypt during the Second Intermediate Kingdom. Egyptians regained power in the New Kingdom, c1550-1070 BCE.

Definition: Hatshepsut

Hatshepsut was one of the ancient world's few female leaders. During the New Kingdom, she was a strong leader. Egypt thrived with an expansion of trade during her reign.

Definition: Kush and Aksum

The Kushites lived south of Upper Egypt in a place called Nubia. Nubia gained power through trade and established an Empire. Under a king named Piankhi, the Kush took control of Egypt and established a dynasty c750 BCE.

Aksum was south of the Kush Empire. Through trade with the Roman Empire and cultures further east, Aksum grew strong and extended through Eastern Africa (centered in modern-day Ethiopia) and into the Arabian Peninsula. They conquered Kush c350 CE. Aksum fell to Muslim invaders c700 CE, and Islam quickly established itself as a religion in Egypt.

Review Questions

1. Early human inhabitants before the Neolithic Revolution tended to
   A) live in nuclear families on the outskirts of cities
   B) congregate in urban areas
   C) live a nomadic lifestyle as they searched for agricultural opportunities
   D) settle closest to the equatorial regions of the continents

2. What type of work is typically done by an archaeologist?
   A) Studying local economies
   B) Analyzing artifacts
   C) Constructing maps
   D) Surveying land

3. The Neolithic Revolution helped to do all of the following EXCEPT:
   A) Create permanent settlements
   B) Lead to the earliest civilizations
   C) Yield more food for farmers to harvest
   D) Increase the demand for Bedouin gatherers in the desert

4. The Fertile Crescent of Mesopotamia is associated with which river?
   A) Ganges
   B) Huang He
   C) Yangtze
   D) Tigris

5. Which of the following is an example of cultural diffusion?
   A) Mesopotamia's soil was fertile enough to grow crops
   B) The Phoenician alphabet was utilized by the Greeks
   C) Nebuchadnezzar destroyed Solomon's Temple
   D) King Hammurabi established a code of law

6. Which of the following was true of Hammurabi's Code?
   A) It was borrowed from the Assyrians
   B) Punishments for the rich and poor were different
   C) Women's rights were enforced
   D) It protected natural rights by limiting the King's power

7. Hieroglyphics of the Egyptians was a writing system which could be compared to cuneiform of the
   A) Israelites
   B) Babylonians
   C) Assyrians
   D) Sumerians

8. Which of the following was true of the Nile in ancient Egypt?
   A) People only lived directly on the banks of the Nile
   B) Water was transferred distances away from the Nile
   C) People did not settle in the Nile Delta out of a fear of floods
   D) The Nile could only be used for transportation because it is composed of salt-water

9. The Egyptian pharaoh ruled in a theocracy. This meant they

A) used military force to gain resources from the Middle East

B) were elected by the people after the death of the previous ruler

C) were established on the behalf of gods

D) allowed the people to have a say in political affairs, but not economic ones

10. Which of the following was true of the rule of Hatshepsut in the New Kingdom of Egypt?

A) Her reign was a failure as it led to the invasion of the Kushites

B) She was successful, as Egypt thrived through extensive trade networks

C) Her rule was the final dynasty of the New Kingdom

D) Egyptians did not tolerate female rule, and she was overthrown

Answers and Explanations

1. **C**. Many early human inhabitants were hunters and gatherers who lived a nomadic lifestyle. They generally moved around in search of food sources.

2. **B**. Archaeologists search and gather artifacts left behind by cultures. Anthropologists are those who study artifacts, and analyze cultures and living conditions.

3. **D**. Many Bedouins, or Middle Eastern nomads, could settle permanently because the Neolithic Revolution led to advances in agriculture. It's important to note that small desert populations of Bedouins still exist today.

4. **D**. The two rivers in Mesopotamia's Fertile Crescent are the Tigris and Euphrates. Mesopotamia is in modern-day Iraq.

5. **B**. The Greek alphabet has similarities to the earlier one used by the Phoenicians. Both alphabets have inspired languages of Western Civilization.

6. **B**. Hammurabi's Code punished the poor harsher than the wealthy.

7. **D**. The Sumerians used clay tablets to record the writing system of cuneiform.

8. **B**. Irrigation networks existed which brought water far away from its source.

9. **C**. A theocracy meant that the pharaoh was ruling as a representative of the gods.

10. **B**. One of the rare female leaders in ancient times, Hatshepsut had a successful and powerful reign.

Asian and Middle Eastern Cultures

East of Egypt, empires began to grow all over Asia and the Middle East. In China, a series of dynasties pushed for technological advancements and cultural achievements. In the Indus River Valley, new Indian empires created magnificent architecture still marveled at today. Similar advances were true of Muslim empires who increased learning through math and science. As empires spread throughout the world, so too did the religion of the conquering powers. Interaction between many cultures took place on trade networks, such as the Silk Roads.

HERE IS WHAT YOU NEED TO KNOW:

• CHINA
Question: Geographically, what rivers of China should I know?

Answer: Much of early Chinese civilization was between the *Yangtze* River in the South, and *Huang He* (Yellow) River in the North. Similar to what was seen in Mesopotamia, people settled near rivers for farming, water, and trade.

Question: What early dynasties should I know about in China?

Answer: A *dynasty* is a chain of family rule. This tends to be *autocratic*, or where total power is centered within the ruler. You should know:

1. Shang Dynasty - c1500-1050 BCE - They mostly lived in the forest. They created wall-like structures for protection, and prayed through oracle bones. These were usually ox bones or tortoise shells which were used to communicate with the gods.

2. Zhou Dynasty - c1100BCE - 221BCE - They made great strides in bronze-making (and later iron), silk, and script (writing). They oper-ated under feudalism. Explained in depth during the Middle Ages chapter, this was a system where land was exchanged for military service so *lords* could maintain their property.

Definition: Mandate of Heaven and The Dynastic Cycle

A *Mandate of Heaven* meant that a ruler was approved by the gods to lead. Because of this, any new leader had to proclaim that they had the Mandate of Heaven. The cycle of where an old leader would lose power, and a new one would rise was called the *Dynastic Cycle*.

In the Dynastic Cycle: A strong dynasty came to power → They declined because of corruption and inner-deterioration → Natural disasters complicated matters and sparked revolts →This led to a dynasty's loss of the Mandate of Heaven →Then an overthrow of the dynasty → Finally, a new dynasty received the Mandate of Heaven and brought peace. Then, the cycle repeated itself.

Definition: Qin Dynasty and Shi Huangdi (Qin Shi Huang)

Shi Huangdi (Qin Shi Huang) called himself the first Emperor of the Qin Dynasty. He doubled the size of China by conquering land. Although much of the Great Wall of China would be built later, an early expansion of the wall was created during his reign. Peasants were forced to construct the wall *to keep out invaders from the north*. Shortly after Huangdi's death in 210 BCE, the Empire declined. Huangdi was buried in a mausoleum in the ancient capital of Xi'an, and was surrounded by an immense army of terra-cotta (clay) soldiers.

The Qin helped implement *Legalism*. Legalism was a belief in a strong government that kept order. It meant that the Emperor should

The Great Wall of China was constructed to keep out foreign invaders from the north

punish those who did not carry out their civil duties. Unlike Confucianism or Daoism, Legalism meant that people had to be disciplined by the government rather than by themselves.

Definition: Han Empire

After the fall of the State of Qin, the Han Dynasty took over China for four centuries. Because the Han lost power for a short amount of time, their reign is divided into the Former/Western Han (202 BCE-9 CE), and the Later/Eastern Han (25-220 CE). *Liu Bang* founded this dynasty.

Question: How did the Han Dynasty control such a large area?

Answer: The Han had a centralized government where many officials controlled the legal policies. Under Emperor Wudi, this evolved into a *bureaucracy*. This means a complex network of government jobs that control a territory. To get a job in the bureaucracy, one had to pass an exam, similar to today's *civil service test*.

The terra-cotta soldiers of Shi Huangdi (Qin Shi Huang)

Question: What were the contributions of the Han Dynasty?

Answer: The reign of the Han was known as a *"golden age"* because of its great contributions. Some of their advances were in:

1. Government - An effective centralized government with civil service jobs.

2. The invention of paper made from trees. This helped spread learning throughout the region. The Han made great strides in math, bot-

any, acupuncture, and astronomy.

3. Farming Equipment - Creation of the wheelbarrow, iron tools, and drainage systems.

Question: What were the innovations of the Tang and the Song?

Answer: Founded by Emperor Tang Taizong, the Tang ruled from 618-907 CE. They took over lands in China, and under Empress Wu Zhao (Wu Zetian), parts of modern-day Korea c700. Zhao was the only female emperor in China's history.

Shortly after the Tang, the Song ruled from 960-1279 CE. It is important to know the contributions of these two dynasties. Their inventions include:

1. Gunpowder - Used at first for fireworks, this was later implemented in weaponry by the Song.

2. Porcelain - Ceramics were made out of heated clay, hence the term, "china."

3. Movable Type - The Tang made block printing, which was a way to copy images. The Song later came out with movable type, where a document's letters and words could be changed at will.

4. Both dynasties used paper money, and the Song's government issued it extensively.

Question: What was the social order of China?

Answer: Beneath the Emperor, there was an upper-class known as the *gentry*. They typically were the educated ones working the government jobs. Next was a middle class of merchants. Finally, the largest group was the peasants. These people typically farmed and worked for the landowning gentry.

As for women, they were viewed as subservient to men. *Foot binding* was commonplace in China. This was when a young girl would have each foot's toes tied to the bottom of the foot. Eventually the foot would break, causing the young woman to shuffle. This was as a symbol of male dominance.

Question: What were the later Chinese Dynasties?

Answer:

1. Ming Dynasty - 1368-1644 - Much of the Great Wall was built by them, as was the Forbidden City, which is a Ming palace/city that still stands in Beijing. You need to know about *Zheng He*. He was an explorer who c1400 traveled the Eastern World on fleets of ships much larger than those used by Europeans a century later.

2. Qing Dynasty - This would be the last dynasty of China. The Manchus were people from the north in Manchuria who invaded. When they conquered, they took on the name Qing. They wanted to keep China self-sufficient and leave it isolated from European influence. They ruled from 1644-1911.

• OTHER EAST ASIA EMPIRES
Question: What is important to know about the Mongol Empire?

Answer:

1. The Mongols were nomadic people who lived on the Steppe (grasslands) of Eastern Europe and Asia.

2. These nomads united under the rule of *Genghis Khan* c1200 CE.

3. Khan conquered much of Eastern Europe and Asia, amassing an Empire greater than that of the ancient Romans. Notably, they conquered Russia and China. The Empire even extended into parts of the Middle East.

4. After Khan's death, the Empire was divided into territories known as Khanates. The Khanate of the Golden Horde contained Russia. In China, they established the Yuan Dynasty. The four Khanates were ruled by one of Khan's

descendants and a series of administrators.

5. Kublai Khan conquered China in 1234, but failed to take over the island of Japan in the late thirteenth century. The Mongols never conquered Japan because upon their invasion, a massive storm known as a *kamikaze* destroyed their fleet of ships.

For about 100 years, there was a Mongol Peace (Pax Mongolica) that ended c1350. The Empire weakened a century after Kublai's death, as famine, rebellion, overexpansion, lack of unified culture, and weak leadership broke up much of the Mongol's landholdings.

6. The Mongols had strong connections with other cultures because of an extensive network of roads and trading routes that extended from India to the Middle East. European traveler Marco Polo visited China c1270. He returned to Italy with reports about Chinese life, communication networks, and the impressive Mongol palaces.

Questions: What do I need to know about early Japan?

Answer: Japan controls a chain of islands known as an *archipelago*. Island geography allowed Japan to isolate itself from the rest of the world for much of its history. Although this isolation protected them from Mongol conquest, it also kept them in a backwards, feudal lifestyle into the nineteenth century.

1. As explained in the religion chapter, the ancient religion was **Shintoism**, which meant "the way of the gods." The religion worshiped ancestors and nature.

2. Much cultural diffusion took place between China, Japan, and Korea. Japanese culture thrived during the Heian Period from 794-1185. Many artistic and literary achievements accompanied this time period.

3. Japan operated on *feudalism* (explained more in depth in the Middle Ages chapter).

Similar to the practice in the Middle Ages where knights gave military service in exchange for land, Japanese **samurai warriors** adhered to the **bushido code**, or "the way of the warrior." Samurais were ready to die if that meant honoring the gods and their obligations.

4. Shogun - Similar to what took place in China, family rule existed in Japan. In 1192, Emperor Minamoto took on the title of Shogun, or dictator.

5. The Tokugawa Shogunate united feudal Japan under military rule c1600. Although they welcomed trade at first, extensive conversions of the Japanese people to Christianity led to rebellion. By 1640, Japan closed its doors to European influence. The isolation would last until the middle of the nineteenth century.

6. In terms of culture, you need to know that **haikus** were three lined poems about nature that traditionally had a 5-7-5 syllable scheme. **Kabuki theater** was a dramatic presentation that featured dance, fancy costumes, and men taking on the roles of women.

Definition: Khmer Empire and Koryu Dynasty

The Khmer Empire dominated Southeast Asia c1200 in what is present-day Cambodia. The capital of the Empire was Angkor. There, an impressive temple complex was constructed called **Angkor Wat**. It was first dedicated to the Hindu god Vishnu, and later became a Buddhist structure. The Khmer Empire established sea-trade with China and India

In Korea, the Koryu Dynasty ruled from 935-1392. Like the Han, they had a bureaucratic government with civil service tests. The Koryu Dynasty declined after Mongol invasions in the thirteenth century.

• INDIA

Question: What geographic features of India are most important to know?

Note: Information on the caste system and Hinduism can be found in the religion chapter.

Answer:

1. Civilization in India developed in the western Indus River Valley near the **Indus River**, and to the east along the **Ganges River**.

2. India's climate is affected by great seasonal winds called **monsoons**. These impressive storms provide the rain necessary for agriculture.

3. Most of the Indian subcontinent is made up of a dry region called the Deccan Plateau.

Remember: **I DIG**...India = **D**eccan, **I**ndus, **G**anges

Definition: Harappa and Mohenjo-Daro

Around 2500 BCE, there were two cities called **Harappa** and **Mohenjo-Daro** in the Indus River Valley. They had a complex city layout, complete with a network of roads and advanced plumbing. By 1700 BCE, nomadic people called **Aryans** took over the area and introduced aspects of Hinduism that would spread throughout the region.

Definition: Mauryan Empire and Gupta Empire

Around 300 BCE, the Mauryan Empire was founded by Chandragupta. It peaked under the reign of his son **Asoka**. Asoka favored Buddhism, but was tolerant of all religions.

For 500 years after Asoka's death there was a power-struggle. The Guptas then took over in 320 CE. The Empire expanded westward and created trade networks within the Mediterranean.

Definition: Silk Roads

These were trade routes that went from China, through India, and into the Middle East and Rome. Spices, metal goods, gold, silk, and many other products made their way from the Eastern World into the West. Because of the popular and valuable silks that came out of China, the path of trade was called the Silk Roads. This network is a great example of cultural diffusion.

Definition: Mughal Empire

The Mughals were a more recent Indian Empire that established itself from 1526-1707. The leaders to know are:

1. Babur - He founded the Empire.

2. **Akbar the Great** - A strong military leader, he conquered territory on both coasts of the subcontinent of India. Akbar was known for preaching **religious tolerance**. Though Muslim, he gave freedoms to many Hindus. During his reign there were also contributions in literature and education.

3. Shah Jahan - He sponsored fantastic architecture like the **Taj Mahal**, which was constructed to honor his late wife Mumtaz Mahal.

4. Aurangzeb - He was an unpopular leader who taxed the people greatly. After overexpansion, the Mughal Empire declined when Europeans began to trade in the area. Soon after, England turned India into the "jewel in its crown" (discussed later).

• MIDDLE EASTERN EMPIRES

Note: A Review of Islam can be found in the religion chapter.

Definition: Caliph

A **caliph** was a religious leader who was also the head of the government. Starting in 632, Abu-Bakr, Umar, and Uthman all became the caliphs who succeeded Muhammad. They were able to take over the Arabian Peninsula in the Middle East. As they expanded their power, they spread Islam.

Question: What early Islamic Empires should I know about?

The Blue Mosque in Istanbul, Turkey. Domes on mosques show similarities to Roman architecture.

Answer:

1. Umayyads - 661-750 - They further spread Islam to the east and west. Although most Muslims accepted Umayyad rule, some did not. The Shi'as believed that the caliph should be a relative of Muhammad. The Sunnis disagreed and stated that rulers could lead as long as they preached his ideas. Still today, these two groups experience violent conflict.

2. Abbasids - 750-1258 - They settled in modern-day Baghdad, Iraq and created a wealthy Empire with a bureaucracy to govern over affairs.

Question: Where else did Islam spread before 1500?

Answer: Through trade and cultural diffusion, Islam spread through the Middle East, into Eastern and Northern (called Maghrib) Africa, and as far as Spain. The Almoravids, Almohads, and other Islamic **Moorish** Empires had a stronghold in Spain from 711 until 1492. In Mali, Africa, a king named Mansa Musa spread Islam throughout his Empire c1300 (explained later).

By the twentieth century, Islam saw great gains in Southeast Asia, notably in Indonesia.

Question: What were the contributions of the early Muslim world?

Answer:

1. Mathematics - Al-Khwarizmi had a new idea in math called al-jabr. This is modern-day algebra.

2. Astronomy - Muslims monitored the stars and planets to make calendars and maps.

3. Calligraphy - This was a style of fancy Arabic (Middle Eastern) handwriting.

4. Architecture - Large and ornate **mosques** were constructed as a place for Islamic wor-

ship. Architecture used in Eastern Europe, such as domes and arches, were borrowed for these mosques. Hence, cultural diffusion from the Greco-Roman world was prevalent. Ornate *mosaics* (art formed from small pieces of stone or glass) were commonly found in mosques.

5. Philosophy - The writings of Averroës blended religion and the philosophy of Aristotle.

Question: What should I know about the Ottoman Empire c1300-1920?

Answer: The Empire was named for Osman I. At its peak, the Ottoman Empire dominated Anatolia, the Balkans, and Northern Africa. Its capital was in Istanbul, previously Constantinople (in modern-day Turkey). As with earlier Islamic empires, religion spread with expansion. *Ghazis* were warriors seen as necessary for such diffusion of religion.

Rulers of the Ottoman Empire were called *sultans*. You need to know *Suleiman the Magnificent*, or Suleiman I. His reign was the true peak of the Empire. By 1530, Suleiman had pushed as far west as Central Europe. *He gave religious freedom to Jews and Christians.* He also devised a law code for political, social, and economic matters. The code coexisted with Sharia (Islamic) law.

Definition: Safavid Empire

From c1501-1722, they were the Shi'a Muslims who conquered Persia (Iran). Their peak occurred under Shah Abbas. Because it was situated in the Middle East, there was great trade with Europe and the Ottoman Empire. After Abbas died, the Empire fell apart in the eighteenth century.

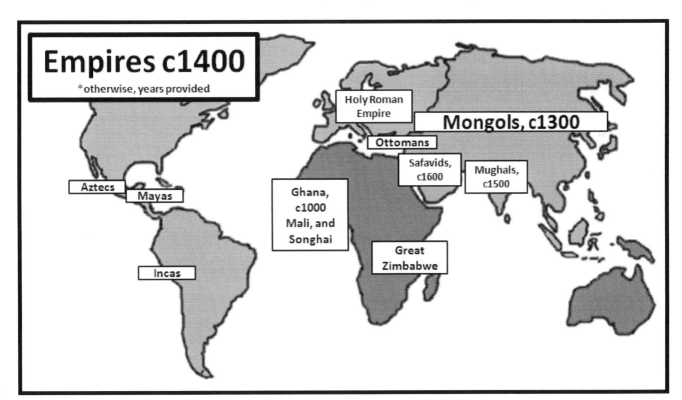

Review Questions

1. Two important rivers of ancient China were the Huang He and the
   A) Ganges
   B) Tigris
   C) Indus
   D) Yangtze

2. All of the following were components of the Dynastic Cycle EXCEPT:
   A) Natural disasters devastating the people
   B) The rise of a new dynasty
   C) Decrease in religious adherence
   D) Revolts of the people

3. The above structure was built to
   A) keep out invaders from the north
   B) prevent people from escaping the country
   C) imprison those who did not pay taxes
   D) act as a dam to control flooding rivers during monsoon season

4. The Han Dynasty c100 BCE, and the Koryu Dynasty c1300 CE, both governed their Empires through
   A) edicts from one dictator
   B) a government bureaucracy based on civil service exams
   C) representative democracy
   D) direct democracy of the local peasants and farmers

5. Which was invented by the Tang and Song Dynasties?
   A) Wheelbarrow
   B) Iron tools
   C) Movable type
   D) Drainage systems

6. Women in ancient China were
   A) often foot bound and kept subservient
   B) allowed to be part of the lawmaking gentry
   C) an important component of the Dynastic Cycle
   D) given the Mandate of Heaven more often than men

7. Which of the following was true of the voyages of Zheng He?
   A) He opened up China to Western trade from England and Spain
   B) His fleet of boats reached North America
   C) His ships were larger and predated European exploration by a century
   D) He discovered the fastest route possible to the West Indies

8. The Mongol Empire never took over parts of
   A) China
   B) Japan
   C) Russia
   D) The Middle East

9. In the Umayyad Caliphate, Shi'a and Sunni Muslims conflicted most over the
   A) interpretation of the Qur'an
   B) length of the holy month of Ramadan
   C) relationship of the caliph to Muhammad
   D) architecture styles used for mosques

10. Both Ottoman ruler Suleiman and Akbar the Great of the Mughal Dynasty
   A) expelled Catholics from Asia Minor
   B) converted to Buddhism
   C) favored the spread of Hinduism throughout Asia and Asia Minor
   D) permitted certain religious freedoms

Answers and Explanations

1. **D**. Today, the Yangtze River is still a major fishing and transportation hub in China.

2. **C**. The Dynastic Cycle was used to explain the transfer of power throughout hundreds of years of Chinese dynasties. Once an Emperor had the Mandate of Heaven, they ruled until their power naturally declined.

3. **A**. The Great Wall was constructed in stages over more than a thousand years. Shi Huangdi was an Emperor who expanded the wall's early construction. It was built to keep out invaders from the north. Over China's history, invasions continued to occur despite the wall.

4. **B**. A bureaucracy is a complex network of specialized government jobs. The Han Dynasty used civil service tests to determine who would work such jobs. A similar bureaucratic testing system (civil service exams) is used today in the United States.

5. **C**. The Tang provided block print, which would print images. The Song went one step further and invented movable type, which allowed a printer to change letters, or different parts of the image.

6. **A**. Women were kept inferior to men in ancient China. It wouldn't be until the twentieth century, mainly during communist rule, that women would see political gains in China.

7. **C**. Zheng He's fleet of ships c1400 was greater than those used in European exploration missions during the fifteenth and sixteenth centuries.

8. **B**. Japan's island geography made it difficult for the Mongols to conquer. A terrible storm wiped out Mongol ships when they attempted to invade.

9. **C**. The dispute was over the relationship of the caliph (religious leader) to Muhammad. Today, these two sects still experience conflict in the Middle East.

10. **D**. Suleiman gave freedoms to non-Muslims within the Ottoman Empire. The same can be said of Akbar the Great of the Mughal Empire.

Greece and Rome

The greatest influence on today's Western Culture of North America and Europe comes from ancient Greece and Rome. Many Western ideas such as government, architecture, literature, math, science, and philosophy, had their roots in Greece. The Romans adopted many of these ideas and spread them throughout their Empire. After Rome fell, the culture was brought East by the Byzantine Empire. Many of the achievements and ideas of the Greco-Roman world have influenced the last two millenniums of global history.

HERE IS WHAT YOU NEED TO KNOW:

• GREECE
Question: How did Greece's geography affect its development?

Answer: Early Greek culture emerged around 2000 BCE near Mycenae. These people were the Mycenaeans.

Mainland Greece is:

1. Mountainous, which made it difficult to link ancient city-states. This led to isolation.

2. Surrounded by water on three sides, which made the peninsula perfect for sea-travel and trade. The Greeks also controlled nearby islands.

Definition: Polis

A polis is a Greek city-state. Major business and government proceedings were conducted atop a hill called an *acropolis*. A polis could function as a:

1. Monarchy - Ruled by a king.
2. Aristocracy - Ruled by wealthy nobles.
3. Oligarchy - Ruled by a powerful and wealthy elite.

Definition: Homer, c750 BCE

Homer wrote epic poems such as the *Iliad* and the *Odyssey*. The *Iliad* was set during the Trojan War between Troy (in Anatolia, or Turkey) and Greek city-states. This is the story where the Greeks hid inside a wooden horse to sneak into Troy. The *Odyssey* portrays the aftermath of the Fall of Troy.

Question: What was the difference between Athens and Sparta?

Answer:

Sparta was a strict military society. From a young age, boys were trained and drilled for military service. It was also an oligarchy, which meant it was ruled by a select few wealthy citizens.

Athens, whose leader was Pericles c450 BCE, supported a *direct democracy*. This meant that many of the local male citizens could govern over the affairs of the polis. Women and slaves had no political power. Education, more than military training, was favored in Athens.

Both Athens and Sparta teamed up to defeat invaders in the Persian Wars from 490-479 BCE. The victory helped Athens usher in a new golden age of culture in the fifth century BCE.

Definition: Peloponnesian War

In 431 BCE, Sparta declared war on the Athenians. Because of Sparta's military advantage, Athens surrendered in 404 BCE. The war devastated the Athenian government and led many to question the efficiency of democracy.

Question: What were some of the cultural accomplishments of the Greeks?

Answer:

1. Classical Art and Architecture - As seen in the Athenian *Parthenon*, symmetry and columns were major components. The famous types of columns to know are Doric (represent-

The Parthenon's symmetry and use of columns makes it an excellent example of classical architecture. Note that restoration of this great piece of history is an ongoing project.

ing strength), Ionic (wisdom), and Corinthian (beauty). Like architecture, Greek sculpture was also symmetrical. It often portrayed cultural events, war scenes, and the human body.

2. Drama - Theatrical performances of both comedies and tragedies were popular.

3. Literature - Besides Homer's poems, writers to know are Sophocles (*Oedipus the King* and *Antigone*), Aeschylus (*The Oresteia*), and Euripides (*Medea*).

4. Philosophy after the Peloponnesian War - A new era of thinking began (explained next).

5. Math - Pythagoras had a famous theorem regarding the triangle, Euclid's *Elements* laid the foundation for geometry, and Archimedes used the measurement of π (pi).

6. Science - Aristarchus studied astronomy and the movement of the planets and sun. Hippocrates made great strides in medicine.

7. Olympics - These games that were once held to honor the god Zeus are still held today for international athletic competition.

Question: Who were the "Big Three" philosophers of Ancient Greece?

Answer: **SPA**

1. **S**ocrates (469-399 BCE) - He believed in questioning the world around him. Socrates stated that "*the unexamined life is not worth living*." The government found him guilty of corrupting the youth of Athens. He was sentenced to death.

2. **P**lato (427-347 BCE) - A student of Socrates, he constructed much of his writings as dialogues between more than one person. He wrote ***The Republic***, where he outlined an efficient government controlled by the most intelligent leaders, or philosopher-kings.

3. **A**ristotle (384-322 BCE) - A student of Plato, he used logic to test sciences such as biology, psychology, and metaphysics. Alexander the Great was one of his students.

Definition: Hellenistic Age

North of Greece is Macedonia. There in

30

359 BCE, Philip II became king. By the time of his assassination in 336 BCE, Macedonia controlled or occupied much of the Greek peninsula. Philip's son, Alexander, declared himself the new king. Alexander the Great, as he would later become known, defeated King Darius III of Persia. After that victory, he marched into Egypt, and spread as far east as India.

After his conquests, a blending of Greek, Persian, Egyptian, and Indian cultures took place. This cultural diffusion was known as *Hellenistic culture*, and the exchanging of ideas occurred in architecture, religion, art, and literature.

• ROME

Question: How did Rome's early republic function?

Answer: A republic is a type of government where the citizens vote for others to represent them. In later centuries, different styles of the Roman Republic would be adopted all over the world. The Roman Republic was comprised of:

1. *Patricians* - The *aristocracy*, or rich property owners who had the most power.

2. *Plebeians* - Commoners such as merchants and farmers. They were not allowed to hold high office. Eventually, in the Roman Senate, they became elected officials called *tribunes*.

3. Senate - Controlled by the aristocracy, this strong legislative group served for life. As mentioned above, plebeians eventually received a voice here.

4. Dictators - The Roman Republic was allowed to appoint a dictator, or absolute ruler, to govern in times of war or conflict.

5. *Twelve Tables of Law*, c450 BCE - These were written laws that expressed individual rights within the Republic. They were displayed at the Roman Forum (meeting center) for all to see.

Question: What was the extent of the Roman Empire before the rise of Julius Caesar?

Answer: Land-owning citizens had to perform mandatory military service in the Roman Legion.

1. The Legions conquered what is now modern-day Italy.

2. Competing for trade in the Mediterranean, Rome fought the *Punic Wars* with Carthage in northern Africa. There were three wars fought between 264-146 BCE.

3. The Second Punic War saw Carthaginian leader *Hannibal* take his troops, horses, and elephants through the French Alps and attack Rome from the north. He never captured Rome, and a Roman general named Scipio defeated him near Carthage.

4. In the third war, Senator Cato's belief that, "Carthage must be destroyed" became a reality when in 146 BCE, it was set on fire. Rome's victory in battle gave them control of the Mediterranean Sea. Less than 100 years later, their Empire expanded from Western Europe to Anatolia (Turkey).

Question: What should I know about Julius Caesar?

Answer:

1. After civil war plagued Rome, Julius Caesar rose to power. He was elected to the high office of consul in 59 BCE, and along with two others comprised a *triumvirate* of rulers.

2. Caesar became a dictator, or absolute ruler, and conquered land in Greece, Western Europe, Egypt, and Asia.

3. He gave citizenship to some in the conquered territories, and preached land reform to aid the poor.

4. He became dictator for life in 44 BCE, but was assassinated shortly thereafter on March 15, 44 BCE...the Ides of March.

Question: What happened after Caesar's assassination?

Answer: Caesar's relative Octavian, along with General Mark Antony, banded together to rule Rome. After the two experienced conflict, Octavian emerged as the true leader of Rome and took on the title of *Augustus*.

Definition: Pax Romana

Pax Romana was a time of about 200 years of peace from 27 BCE to 180 CE. It coincided with the rise of Augustus. This tranquil period led to greater expansion of the Roman Empire, vast trade, and cultural advances.

Question: What cultural advancements of Rome should I know?

Answer:

1. The great architectural project of the Roman Colosseum provided a meeting center for entertainment. Gladiators were known to fight to the death in this arena. On smaller structures, domes were used by the Romans to create vaulted ceilings.

2. As stated earlier, you need to know about the Twelve Tables of Law.

3. *Aqueducts* were stone and concrete structures, typically on arches, that distributed water to the population. In addition, an impressive network of roads linked the Empire.

4. Virgil's *Aeneid* was modeled after the epics of the Greeks. Such cultural diffusion of the Greeks was common in Rome. Roman literature, art, and architecture all showed Greek influence. This combination of Greco-Roman culture laid the foundation for *Western Civilization*, or *Western Culture* in Europe.

5. As stated in the religion chapter, Christianity spread through the Roman Empire. In 313 CE, persecution of Christians ended after Emperor Constantine won a battle which he attributed to Christianity. The Edict of Milan

The arches of the Roman Colosseum

promoted religious tolerance.

Question: What led to the Fall of Rome?

Answer: Rome fell in 476 CE. It collapsed because of economic issues such as inflation and failing agriculture, and political factors such as overexpansion.

A century earlier, Emperor Constantine moved the capital of the Empire eastward from Rome to Byzantium (Constantinople). This also hastened the decline of Rome. After invasions from tribes such as the Huns (first led by Attila), Rome weakened from famine and political unrest. In the end, the depleted Empire fell quietly.

Question: What should I know about the New Rome of Byzantium?

Answer: The Eastern Roman Empire survived as the Byzantine Empire. You need to know about Emperor Justinian. Justinian:

1. Established a code of Roman law c530 CE. Justinian's Code contained social laws expanding the rights of women (marriage rights)

and slaves. It also provided laws against *heresy* (clashing with the established religion).

2. He supported a unification of church and state. His most ornate Church, the Hagia Sophia, eventually became a mosque when the Ottoman Empire conquered Constantinople (now called Istanbul).

Question: What happened to Christianity in the Byzantine Empire in 1054?

Answer: There was a *schism*, or split. This East-West schism occurred partly because there was a controversy over the use of *icons*, or images used in prayer, in the Eastern parts of the Byzantine Empire. From Rome, Emperor Leo III declared icons to be synonymous with idol worship.

As the religious practices of Eastern and Western Europe drifted apart, there was an eventual split where the Eastern faction became *Eastern Orthodox*, while the Western one continued to practice *Roman Catholicism*.

Question: How did Byzantine culture affect Russia?

1. Vladimir the Great and Yaroslav the Wise supported adopting Eastern Orthodox Christianity for the Russian people, notably in Kiev. Kiev was a center of trade for Russians, Vikings, and northern Slavic people.

2. The Mongol Empire controlled the Russian people for over 250 years.

3. When Russia became independent from Mongol rule in 1480, influences of Byzantine culture were still present. One example is the *Cyrillic alphabet*, which has connections to Slavic people who traded in Constantinople. Many Russians had a Slavic heritage.

Review Questions

1. How did geography influence the development of the Greek polis before 500 BCE?

  A) Flatlands led to immense cultural diffusion throughout the peninsula

  B) Mountains isolated individual city-states

  C) The Romans were able to conquer Greece in 400 BC because of its position on the Aegean Sea

  D) Greece's open terrain made it an easy target for Persian conquest

2. The Golden Age of Athens came after which conflict?

  A) First Punic War

  B) Persian Wars

  C) Peloponnesian War

  D) Trojan War

3. Which of the following best describes Spartan society?

  A) Immense concentration on art and architecture

  B) Development of a disciplined military-state

  C) Presence of an absolute monarchy

  D) Promotion of a direct democracy

4. The philosophy of Socrates can best be described as

  A) a belief in a republic controlled by a philosopher king

  B) great research in biology and metaphysics

  C) asking questions to discover the truth

  D) arguments for rigid class structure

5. Which of the following best classifies Pax Romana?

  A) A time when the Twelve Tables of Law established women's rights

  B) Pericles' creation of a direct democracy

  C) Julius Caesar's extension of the Roman Empire into India

  D) A lasting peace that helped develop culture

6. Aqueducts were important to the Roman Empire because they

  A) improved the architecture of Catholic Churches

  B) helped to distribute water to the Empire

  C) provided a defense from invading tribes from the north

  D) became a means for trading on the Silk Roads

7. The end of religious persecutions against Christians within the Roman Empire coincided with

  A) the early years of Pax Romana

  B) Octavian's rise to power

  C) the fall of the Empire

  D) a military victory by Emperor Constantine

8. All of the following were causes for the Fall of Rome in 476 CE EXCEPT:

  A) Overexpansion of the Empire

  B) Corruption of public officials

  C) An increase in taxes

  D) Decay of the infrastructure of Roman roads

9. Which of the following was true of Justinian's Code?

A) It increased rights among women

B) New prayer rituals were instituted for Muslims

C) Christian prayer was made illegal inside the Hagia Sophia

D) It was the first code of law ever created by an Empire

10. The Byzantine Empire was different from Rome in all of the following ways EXCEPT:

A) Language

B) Greek heritage

C) Religious practice

D) Trade partners

Answers and Explanations

1. **B**. Greece is a mountainous peninsula. Mountains made it difficult for the Greeks to unite, and led to the creation of independent city-states. An ancient Greek city-state is referred to as a polis.

2. **B**. Greek victory in the Persian Wars (490-479 BCE) ushered in a Golden Age of cultural achievement.

3. **B**. Whereas Athens concentrated more on cultural achievement, the Spartans were a disciplined military state.

4. **C**. Socrates believed that "the unexamined life is not worth living." He questioned as a way to create dialogue and analysis. This *Socratic Method* is still used today.

5. **D**. Pax Romana was the Roman peace. It strengthened the Empire and led to cultural advancements within Rome.

6. **B**. Aqueducts were stone structures built on arches that helped distribute water to areas within, and outside of, Rome.

7. **D**. Once before a battle, Emperor Constantine had visions of crosses in the sky. After the subsequent military victory, he ended the persecution of Christians with the Edict of Milan.

8. **D**. There were many causes for the Fall of Rome. However, Roman roads are still present today in Italy and elsewhere. A great number of them were still intact by 476 CE.

9. **A**. Justinian's Code, though not the first code in the history of the world, gave more rights to women within the Byzantine Empire.

10. **B**. Although the Byzantine Empire was considerably east of Rome, they still maintained a Greek heritage similar to the Romans.

Middle Ages, Renaissance, and the Protestant Reformation

After the Fall of Rome, Western Europe went into intellectual decline. The Middle Ages, or Medieval Period, saw a fragmented Europe that mostly operated under a system of feudalism. Complicating matters were the harsh realities of war and disease. However, these Dark Ages gave way to the Renaissance where Europe experienced a rebirth and flowering of culture. This rebirth was also accompanied by controversy. When Martin Luther hammered the 95 Theses to the Church at Wittenberg, a shockwave was sent throughout the religious establishment of Europe. The Protestant Reformation would lead to new religious sects by the seventeenth century.

HERE IS WHAT YOU NEED TO KNOW:

• THE MIDDLE AGES
Definition: Middle Ages

"The Middle Ages" are what historians call the time period in Europe between roughly 500-1500. This was an era when Europe slowly evolved after the Fall of Rome. Because of a slow growth in intellectual thought, parts of this time are referred to as the Dark Ages. A synonym for Middle Ages is *Medieval*.

Definition: Carolingian Dynasty/Charlemagne

The Franks were Germanic people from Gaul (France). Their first Christian king was Clovis. When he died, Charles "The Hammer" Martel took over. Then his son, Pepin the Short, was given the title of "King by the Grace of God." This began the Carolingian Empire.

Pepin's son was *Charlemagne*. Under his reign from 768-814, the Carolingian Empire controlled more land than the Byzantines.

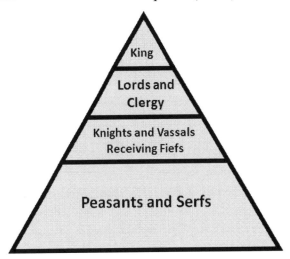

Charlemagne's Frankish Kingdom conquered or controlled areas in Central, Eastern, and Western Europe. Charlemagne was crowned Holy Roman Emperor in 800. Charlemagne's title inspired the Holy Roman Empire, which dominated Central Europe for centuries beginning c1000.

Definition: Feudalism

The Middle Ages were a harsh time where invaders (Vikings, Magyars, and Muslims) looked to plunder European lands.

Feudalism was a political and economic system that involved land ownership and military service. Feudalism was strong in most of Europe until about 1500. It was still prominent in Japan into the nineteenth century.

The general pyramid of feudalism involved a king on top, followed by nobles known as lords. Beneath were *knights* who protected the lord's *manor*, or estate. Some knights received a fief (piece of land) for their service and were known as vassals. At the bottom of the pyramid were tax-paying peasants and serfs. *Serfs* were bound to the land, and could not travel. Serfdom existed in Russia until the nineteenth century, when Czar Alexander II emancipated (freed) them.

King

Lords and Clergy

Knights and Vassals Receiving Fiefs

Peasants and Serfs

Definition: Chivalry

Chivalry was a code of conduct where a knight fought honorably for the lord and his lady. This was similar to the Japanese *bushido code* of the *samurai warrior*.

Chivalry affected the way knights treated women. Though not equals, women were seen in a pure and virtuous light. *Troubadours*, or musicians in castles, sang about the themes of love and honor.

Question: What should I know about the Middle Age economy?

Answer:

1. It was mostly agricultural, with a *Three Field System* whereby land would be farmed in sections. One of those sections would be left unfarmed so the soil could rejuvenate.

2. Many worked in business and were artisans. The merchant class was known as *burghers*. *Guilds*, similar to today's unions, protected the working rights of artisans of a similar craft. The guild members were *masters* of their trade. Before becoming a master, one had to be an *apprentice* for another master, and then a wage-earning *journeyman*.

3. In Northern Europe near the Baltic Sea, there was a commercial organization known as the *Hanseatic League*. States in modern-day Germany, Sweden, Poland, Latvia, Estonia, and others formed this organization to protect trading rights such as freedom of the seas, and fair weights and measures. The League was strong from the thirteenth through seventeenth centuries.

Question: What should I know about the Roman Catholic Church of the Middle Ages?

Answer: Because the Church was incredibly important and powerful, the Middle Ages was also known as the *Age of Faith*. You should know:

1. The Church was in charge of giving out *sacraments* (sacred rites) which were necessary for *salvation*, or going to heaven. The Church's clergy was comprised of first the Pope, then archbishops and bishops, and finally local priests. The law of the church was called canon law.

2. *Lay investiture* - This was when kings and rich nobles appointed religious officials. This would give them an unfair influence over the Church. Though the Church was powerful, activities such as lay investiture were viewed by many as corrupt.

3. *Excommunication* - This meant to kick one out of the Church.

4. The Church struggled for power with the Holy Roman Emperors. At the Concordat of Worms in 1122, the Pope and Emperor compromised their issues.

5. Still, corruption continued. *Simony* occurred when Church positions were sold.

6. Churches were in Romanesque and *Gothic* architecture styles. Romanesque churches were symmetrical with rounded arches and towers. Gothic churches were ornate with pointed arches, stained-glass windows, and *flying buttresses* that linked walls. (See photo of St. Vitus's Cathedral in Prague on next page.)

7. Some attacked the church, such as John Wycliffe and Jan Hus. Around 1380, Wycliffe said that Jesus Christ was the true head of the Church, not the Pope. Around 1400, Hus preached that the Bible was of a higher authority than the Pope. Hus was excommunicated and burned at the stake.

Definition: The Crusades, 1095-1291

These were religious wars fought between European Christians and Muslims from Africa and Asia Minor (Anatolia/Turkey). Both were fighting to secure the Holy Land of Jerusalem. In total, there were nine Crusades. You don't

St. Vitus's Cathedral in Prague is a gothic church with pointed arches, flying buttresses, and stained-glass windows

need to know all of them, but you should know:

1. The First Crusade was called for by Pope Urban II in 1095. The Crusaders were mainly Roman Catholic armored knights with crosses on their shields. They briefly captured land near Jerusalem, but could not hold onto it. Turks from the former **Seljuk Empire of Anatolia** prevented a Crusader victory.

2. In the Second Crusade, Jerusalem was taken by the Muslim commander **Saladin**. In the Third Crusade, Crusader and English King **Richard the Lionheart** reached an agreement that allowed Christians to enter the Holy Land as visitors in 1192.

3. Though violent and creating much religious strife, the Crusades created new trade networks between Europe, Asia, and Northern Africa. Not only were goods and innovations exchanged, but scientific and mathematical thought as well.

4. The Crusades further weakened the system of feudalism, as money became more valuable and cities began to rise.

Definition: Spanish Inquisition

This was a movement in Spain that looked to maintain the orthodoxy of the country through forced conversions and deportation. A tribunal interrogated those seen as heretics (people with beliefs that clashed with the Catholic Church). Typically the oppressed were Jews, Muslims, or recent converts to Christianity. Confessions were often forced through torture. Remnants of the inquisition existed into the nineteenth century.

The Inquisition came amidst the **Reconquista**, which was a plan to remove Muslims from Spain. Christians kicked out the remaining Muslim kingdoms in 1492. For about the previous 800 years, the Moors (Muslim invaders from northern Africa) had conquered much of the Iberian Peninsula (Spain and Portugal).

Definition: Thomas Aquinas and Dante Alighieri

Aquinas was a religious scholar who wrote the *Summa Theologica* c1274. His work is a combination of Christian theology (study of religious faith) and Greek philosophical thought, specifically from Aristotle. Aquinas' followers were called **scholastics**.

Dante Alighieri's *Divine Comedy* is an epic poem from c1321 that portrays a soul's journey. The book travels through Hell, Purgatory, and Heaven. In the book, Dante incorporates some of the same religious philosophy used by Aquinas.

Definition: Great Schism, 1378-1417

Unlike the schism of 1054 that divided religion between Eastern Orthodox and Roman Catholicism, this schism was *within* the Catholic Church. Two people declared themselves Pope; Pope Urban VI in Rome, and Clement VII in Avignon, France. Eventually, a different Pope was elected.

Definition: Bubonic Plague/Black Death

Approximately one-third of Europe's population died of this dreaded disease. The plague was believed to be brought to Italy from Asia in 1348. It then spread to the entire continent. The Black Death ultimately hurt the prestige of the Church as prayers went unanswered. The plague further weakened the stability of the feudal system.

Definition: Hundred Years' War, 1337-1453

England and France had a history of conflict. In 1066, **William the Conqueror** from Northern France (Normandy) took the English throne. His descendants continued to rule England. That included King Henry II, who married Eleanor of Aquitaine. She had been a wife to both an English and French King.

This war wasn't really 100 years. But from 1337-1453 England and France were engaged in battle. In the war, a French girl named **Joan of Arc** saw visions from God and felt compelled to save France. Although Joan led the army to victory, she was later captured and accused of heresy and witchcraft. She was burned at the stake in 1431.

The Hundred Years' War was mostly a standoff, as England won very little territory by war's end.

• THE RENAISSANCE
Definition: Renaissance

This was a time period from about 1350-1550 that saw a "rebirth" of learning and culture. There was also a push for individualism, as unlike those born into wealth, a new merchant and artistic class believed that one should be judged by achievements. The movement affected art, literature, political thought, and science.

Question: Where did the Renaissance begin?

Answer: Italy. Italy borders the Mediterranean, and is a perfect port for economic commerce and trade. In addition, Italy's social roots were based on the classical traditions of Greco-Roman culture. The Italian Renaissance was centered in Florence where the influential Medici family ruled the city by 1434.

Definition: Humanism

Humanism was a cultural and philosophical movement that celebrated a person's achievements. Whereas the Middle Ages stressed studying Christianity, humanism looked to investigate the classical teachings of ancient Greece and Rome. Humanists expanded education in subjects called humanities (social studies, literature, philosophy, languages). They wanted to **secularize** society, or make it worldly instead of religious.

Question: What should I know about Renaissance Art?

Answer: Whereas Medieval art was concerned with religious themes that were often out of proportion, many of the Renaissance paintings were secular and done in **realism**. This meant breathtaking detailed images proportional to the human body. Renaissance art was colorful and done in perspective, or three dimensions. Some artists to know are:

1. Michelangelo - His statue of the *David* was completed in 1504 and today can be found in Florence. The statue is both a symbol of strength and a celebration of the human

A replica of Michelangelo's David *stands in Florence for all to see*

body. Michelangelo also painted the ceiling of the Sistine Chapel in Rome (Vatican City). He sculpted the *Pietà* which portrays the Virgin Mary holding her son Jesus after the crucifixion. The statue is currently at St. Peter's Basilica in Vatican City.

2. Raphael - He painted *Madonna and Child*. He also painted the *School of Athens*, which is a c1510 masterpiece where Plato walks with Aristotle. It is a *fresco*, which is a work of art painted on damp plaster, typically on walls.

3. Leonardo da Vinci - c1500, he was truly a "Renaissance Man," as his talents went beyond art. Among other things he was an inventor, scientist, sculptor, and writer. His best known paintings were the *Mona Lisa* and *The Last Supper*. In both, one can sense the emotions of the subjects.

4. Donatello - He was a sculptor who also was able to convey emotions into stone.

5. Outside of Italy, Flemish painter Jan van Eyck was successful using oil paints. In Germany, Albrecht Dürer and Hans Holbein were famous for their paintings of realism that brought people to life.

Definition: Gutenberg's Printing Press, c1440

Literature became more widely available because of *Johann Gutenberg's* invention of the printing press. The *Gutenberg Bible* was one of the earliest works printed in Europe. Because of this new use of movable type, learning spread throughout Europe at a much faster pace. Further increasing education, many writers abandoned Latin and wrote books in *vernaculars*, or local/native tongues.

Question: What should I know about Renaissance literature?

Answer:

1. Niccolò Machiavelli wrote *The Prince* in 1513. In this work he explained that a strong leader must rule harshly to keep order. Otherwise, people would walk all over that leader. Therefore, a ruthless personality is needed to not only secure power, but hold onto it.

2. The *Elizabethan Age* refers to the reign of Queen Elizabeth where great literature was being produced in England (explained next).

3. Thomas More wrote *Utopia* which is a commentary about a fictitious, perfect, and peaceful place.

Definition: Elizabethan Age

This refers to the Renaissance period in England that coincided with the reign of Queen Elizabeth I from 1558-1603. Elizabeth Tudor was a patron of the arts who sponsored artistic endeavors. During this time, William Shakespeare of England wrote and produced comedies such as *The Merchant of Venice*, and tragedies like *Hamlet* and *Macbeth*.

Note: The Renaissance experienced in Eng-

land, France, and Germany is known as the **Northern Renaissance**.

• PROTESTANT REFORMATION
Question: What was the Protestant Reformation?

Answer: This was a movement by people who _protest_ed, and wanted to reform (change for the better) the Roman Catholic Church. From 1517 through the next century, new sects of Christianity were formed.

Question: What were the causes of the Reformation?

Answer: For centuries there had been critics of the Roman Catholic Church, such as John Wycliffe and Jan Hus during the Middle Ages. By 1500, the causes for discontent were:

1. Selling of _indulgences_. An indulgence allowed people to sin without being punished. Dominican priest Johann Tetzel sold these pardons to raise money to renovate St. Peter's Cathedral in Rome.

2. Resentment to the power of the Pope and clergy.

3. A belief that the Bible was far more important than the power of church officials.

Definition: Martin Luther/95 Theses

On October 31, 1517, a religious monk named Martin Luther hammered a list of grievances to a church in Wittenberg, Germany. These were the _95 Theses_. They were quickly copied and distributed throughout Germany and Western Europe. The main ideas of the Theses were that:

1. The Bible was the authority of Christianity, not the clergy.

2. Only God could give salvation to heaven.

3. To get into heaven, one must have faith and do good deeds/works.

4. Church practices created during the Middle Ages were not binding.

Luther also attacked the selling of indulgences. These ideas helped start the Protestant Reformation.

Question: What was the Church's reaction to Luther's ideas?

Answer: Pope Leo X excommunicated Luther (kicked him out of the Church) when he refused to take back his words.

In 1521, Luther stood trial in front of the Diet (assembly) of Worms at Worms, Germany. Again, he wouldn't retract his statements. Holy Roman Emperor Charles V issued the Edict of Worms, which labeled Luther a heretic. It also banned his writings and ideas. Still, _Lutherans_ followed his teachings.

Question: What was the immediate impact of the Reformation in Germany?

Answer: As people began to preach Luther's teachings, violence ensued as peasants revolted in Germany looking for more political rights. In addition, German princes were divided as to which religion to support. Eventually, Holy Roman Emperor Charles V was able to bring peace between the Catholic and Protestant princes. In the 1555 _Peace of Augsburg_, the princes agreed to allow the ruler of each German state to determine if it would be Catholic or Protestant.

Question: Why did Henry VIII of England abandon the Roman Catholic Church?

Answer: The Church did not allow Catholics like Henry to divorce. He decided to break away from the Church, and in 1534, Parliament (the legislature of England) passed the _Act of Supremacy_. This made Henry the head of the Church of England. Because he was now independent of Rome, Henry could divorce his wife, Catherine.

Henry married six women in total. His second wife, Anne Boleyn, was accused of adultery and executed. Earlier, she gave birth to a daughter…who later became Queen Elizabeth I. For generations, England had religious conflicts between Protestants and Catholics.

Question: What should I know about the family tree of Henry VIII?

Answer: Henry had a son who ruled for six years. His first daughter, Mary, favored Catholicism during her reign and put to death many Protestants (hence her nickname, Bloody Mary). After Mary, Elizabeth I took the throne and brought England back to Protestantism. She became the head of the *Anglican Church of England*.

Definition: Calvinism and Predestination

Many different sects of Protestantism evolved. It is important to know about Calvinism.

Influenced by the teachings of John Calvin, Calvinists preach *predestination*, or the concept that God has planned the fate of all people. This means that only certain souls can find salvation. Calvinist principles spread to France, Netherlands, and Switzerland. It was also adopted by Presbyterians in Scotland.

Question: I'm confused – on a map, who is what religion?

Answer: Protestants lived in every country in Europe. However, you should know these generalizations c1600:

Protestant - England, Germany, Austria, Hungary, and Scandinavia (Norway and Sweden)

Roman Catholicism - Spain, France, Italy, and Ireland

Eastern Orthodox - Greece and Russia

Definition: Counter-Reformation/Catholic Reformation

This was an attempt by the Catholic Church to reform itself and keep church members from leaving. Beginning in 1545 at the *Council of Trent*, Catholics condemned indulgences, and reaffirmed the importance of the Bible. Like Luther, they also agreed that good works, as well as faith, were necessary for salvation.

One of the most influential reformers was Ignatius of Loyola. His followers became the Society of Jesus, or *Jesuits*. Their goal was to spread the teachings of Jesus and convert people to Catholicism. To a degree, they were successful in slowing the spread of Protestantism.

Question: What were the results of the Protestant Reformation?

Answer: The major outcome was division between religious sects. Furthermore, the Roman Catholic Church, which had been so powerful during the Middle Ages/Age of Faith, was negatively impacted.

Review Questions

1. Which Carolingian in 800 was the first to be crowned Holy Roman Emperor?
   A) Henry VIII
   B) Richard I
   C) Charlemagne
   D) Alexander the Great

2. The Medieval practice of lay investiture within the Catholic Church involved
   A) kings and nobles appointing religious officials
   B) selling sacraments which would lead to salvation
   C) forcefully removing a member from the Church
   D) enforcing strict interpretation of the Bible

3. A result of the Crusades was
   A) peace in the Middle East for centuries
   B) an increase in cultural diffusion
   C) European control of Jerusalem
   D) revolutions in France

4. The Reconquista was a movement to
   A) expel Jews from the Roman Empire and distribute them across Europe
   B) recapture the Holy Land in and around Jerusalem
   C) convert those seen as heretics to Protestantism
   D) reclaim Spain from centuries of Muslim influence

5. Unlike the schism of 1054, the Great Schism that began in 1378
   A) created the new religion of Eastern Orthodox
   B) united the Church of both the East and the West
   C) involved a dispute as to who was the true Pope
   D) divided power between the Holy Roman Emperor and the Church

6. Renaissance art and literature
   A) moved away from Greco-Roman traditions and styles
   B) originated in England, then moved through Central Europe
   C) lacked emotion and realism
   D) celebrated humanism, and individual achievement

7. Johann Gutenberg's influence on the Renaissance included the
   A) creation of fresco paintings
   B) spreading of the written word throughout Europe
   C) introduction of Flemish painting styles
   D) questioning of the importance of religion

8. The selling of indulgences c1500 was unpopular to many because it meant
   A) one could sin, yet avoid punishment
   B) church officials would be appointed based upon wealth
   C) nobles, who were outside of the Church, could gain clergy offices
   D) the Holy Roman Emperor would control the Church instead of the Pope

9. Martin Luther's 95 Theses were written

A) in response to the declining faith of Catholics

B) to promote religion after its decline during the years of the Black Plague

C) in protest to practices he found corrupt within the Catholic Church

D) on behalf of Calvinists looking to break away from the Church

10. Henry VIII became the head of the Church of England c1534 because he

A) hoped to secure land in Italy which was controlled by the Church

B) wanted to get a divorce from his wife and Rome would not allow it

C) was denied sacraments needed for salvation

D) had a deeply religious adherence to Lutheranism

Answers and Explanations

1. **C**. Charlemagne, King of the Franks, was crowned as the first Holy Roman Emperor in 800.

2. **A**. Lay investiture meant giving kings and nobles the power to appoint church officials. This was one of several Church practices seen as corrupt.

3. **B**. Odd that war would lead to trade. But that was the case for the Crusades. This is an important fact to know.

4. **D**. Muslims had a strong presence in Spain for centuries. The Reconquista looked to drive them out, and reclaim the country for Roman Catholicism. The last Muslims left in 1492.

5. **C**. During the Great Schism there were two men who claimed to be Pope. One was in Rome, and one was in Avignon, France.

6. **D**. Humanism was a big component of Renaissance culture. It celebrated human achievement and stressed Greco-Roman culture.

7. **B**. Gutenberg's printing press spread the written word throughout Europe.

8. **A**. Indulgences were purchased as a pardon from sin. This was heavily criticized by those who wanted to reform the Catholic Church.

9. **C**. In 1517, Martin Luther hammered the 95 Theses to a church in Wittenberg, Germany. He was protesting what he believed to be corruption within the Church.

10. **B**. Under Church law, Henry VIII could not get a divorce from his wife. To get around this, he became the head of the Church of England and granted himself the divorce.

Africa, Native America, and the Age of Exploration

African and Native American Empires thrived for centuries. Kingdoms in Western Africa depended on a valuable gold-salt trade. Culturally diverse because of its challenging geography, Africans had contact with different cultures from Europe to the Middle East. Unlike Africans, Native Americans were isolated from the rest of the globe living in what would become known as the New World. Much of their history and culture is still a mystery to the Western World. However, their impressive architectural creations and cultural symbols still impress historians and tourists alike. The Age of Exploration brought Europeans to the New World, and within decades, the Empires of Native America were destroyed. Europeans extracted great wealth from these new lands. Explorers would capitalize on Africa as well, especially in the coming centuries.

HERE IS WHAT YOU NEED TO KNOW:

• AFRICA

Question: How diverse is Africa's climate?

Answer: Very. The various climate zones include:

1. Desert - The Sahara is the largest desert in the world. It experiences hot temperatures and dry soil. The desert has been expanding southward to a region called the *Sahel*. When grassy regions dry up, it's called *desertification*.

2. Savannah - A wet and dry climate which creates tall grassy plains that support agriculture.

3. Rain Forest - The middle of the continent has a wet climate with an abundance of trees. People do not typically populate the jungles near the Equator.

4. Steppe - Extreme temperatures and little rainfall.

5. Mediterranean - High temperatures with wet winters and autumns.

Question: What was early African society like?

Answer:

1. Nomadic people formed clans, or small groups. Rather than living in nuclear families (with just parents and children), people typically resided with extended families (grandparents, aunts, uncles, etc).

2. Most were *hunters and gatherers*, as men hunted and women gathered vegetation.

3. An early religion was *animism*, which believed in the spirits that existed in nature (see religion chapter).

4. Some families were patrilineal, meaning they traced ancestry through the father. The opposite would be matrilineal, as some societies traced it through the mother.

Definition: Bantu-Speaking People

Because of the diversified geography, many different cultures emerged south of the Sahara Desert. However, tribal languages had similarities because they derived from the migrations of the *Bantu* people as early as 2000 BCE. Many of today's African languages date back to these ancient travelers.

Question: What African Empires should I know c800-1500?

Answer: The most important early trade network in Africa was the *gold-salt* exchange. Western Africa had abundant gold, but a lack of salt. You should know the following Kingdoms of Africa's West Coast:

1. Ghana, c800-c1050 - They grew rich from their trade of gold. There was much cultural diffusion with the Muslim world.

2. Mali, c1200-c1450 - **Mansa Musa** was a powerful King. He performed the hajj, **and brought Islam into the Empire**.

3. Songhai, c1400-c1600 - Controlling the trading city of Timbuktu, Songhai was the largest Empire in Western Africa.

4. Hausa - They built city-states c1000 in modern-day Nigeria. They traded with Africa and Europe…as did the Benin culture.

5. You should also know Axum and Kush, as explained in the second chapter. They were trading centers near Egypt that linked Africa and the Mediterranean.

6. In Eastern Africa, because of contact with Middle Eastern countries, a new language called **Swahili** emerged. This is a combination of African Bantu and Arabic. Contact was strong between Arabia and Eastern African Empires like Zimbabwe and the Mutapa. Zimbabwe had impressive stone wall enclosures that were used for defense. Muslims in the region also traded for slaves in Eastern Africa. (See *Empires c1400* map on pg. 25.)

Definition: Ibn Battuta

He was a North African traveler who ventured for 29 years throughout the African and Muslim world. He also went as far as Asia, and Eastern and Western Europe. His observations are of interest to those comparing the strengths of World Empires, and cultural diversity in the mid-fourteenth century.

• NATIVE AMERICA
Question: Who were the first Native American people?

Answer: During the Ice Age, people traveled over a land bridge known as Beringia that connected Asia to North America (Alaska). These migrants settled and populated what would become known as the *New World*. They lived as hunters and gatherers, and were especially good farmers. They grew **maize** (corn) in particular.

Question: What were the early Native American Empires?

Answer:

1. Olmec - c1200-c400 BCE - Earliest civilization in Mesoamerica (Mexico). Many historians believe they were the first society in North America to have a writing system. They most likely worshipped jaguars.

2. Zapotec - c1000 BCE - Western Mesoamerican culture that had some vast building structures such as pyramids and religious centers.

3. Chavín - c900-c200 BCE - Populating the Andes Mountains in South America, they had advanced canals and drainage systems.

4. Nazca - c200 BCE-500 CE - Living in the dry lands of Peru, they created elaborate irrigation systems. Mysterious lines detailing insects and animals still highlight the area.

5. Moche - c200 CE - They used rivers for irrigation and established a strong agricultural society.

6. Anasazi - c3000 BCE-900 CE - They lived in the modern-day American Southwest. They constructed **pueblos**, or cities made from adobe architecture (clay-bricked).

7. Northwestern Native Americans used totems, or totem poles, to represent a family or group in the community.

Question: What should I know about the Mayan Empire?

Answer: The Mayans lived in Mesoamerica, peaking from about 250-900 CE. Some of their cities were Tikal in Guatemala, and Chichen Itza in the Yucatán Peninsula of Mexico.

1. They built elaborate cities. In Chichen Itza, there were pyramids, a ball court, and an observatory.

2. They had a great understanding of math and astronomy.

3. They had a written language composed of glyphs, or symbols. The books were called codices (or codex for singular).

4. Their most celebrated work was the Popol Vuh, which is their story of creation.

5. Once a great civilization, they mysteriously began to shrink in numbers. Some historians think there was war. Others believe there was a plague or famine.

Question: What should I know about the Aztec Empire?

Answer: The Aztecs lived in Mexico, near modern-day Mexico City. An early city was Teotihuacan. The Aztecs took it over after the fall of the Toltecs.

1. Teotihuacan established trade networks. One item traded was a razor-sharp rock known as obsidian. Obsidian was used to cut out the hearts of sacrifices to the sun god Huitzilopochtli.

2. Another major deity to know in Mesoamerica was Quetzalcoatl, the Feathered Serpent.

3. Tenochtitlan, near Lake Texcoco, was a major Aztec city with palaces and pyramids.

4. The Aztec Empire expanded by 1400 but then weakened under Montezuma II in the sixteenth century.

5. Montezuma and the Aztecs fell to the Spanish (explained later). Many Aztecs believed that the Spanish were Quetzalcoatl.

Question: What should I know about the Inca Empire?

Answer:

1. The Incas had a vast Empire in western South America along the *Andes Mountains*. They were strong in Peru. Mountain ranges like the Andes are visible on *physical maps*, which color and depict the Earth's land features.

2. There was great observance to the sun god, Inti.

3. Immense stone structures displayed advanced architectural skills. Notably, the impressive city of Machu Picchu is today a tourist attraction in Peru. The city of Cuzco was a cultural center. Many of the structures in the city were draped with gold. Some Incan structures were constructed from large stones that did not use mortar to fasten them. They instead fit together like puzzle pieces.

4. The Incas had an organized government and a strong network of roads. There was a labor system called Mita. This meant public service, or citizens aiding in construction.

5. Because it was in the mountains, there was a need for *terrace farming* (explained next).

6. Like the other Native American Empires, the Incas were conquered by the Europeans (explained later).

Incas built impressive structures with stones that often fit together like puzzle pieces. No mortar was used.

Definition: Terrace Farming

Farming done in the mountains meant that crops had to be harvested in a certain manner. Terraces were like steps that went up a mountain. This allowed farming to be done on the slopes of the Andes. In addition, when it rained, water and nutrients would be washed down the steps, as opposed to running off. Terrace farm-

Terraces were used for agriculture in the Andes

ing was used all over the world where sloped terrain was present.

• THE AGE OF EXPLORATION
Question: Why did Europeans want to explore the New World?

Answer: **GGG** (see below). The Age of Exploration was from roughly 1492-1700. New technologies in shipbuilding emerged. The Portuguese built *caravels*, which were small fast-moving boats with large sails. An *astrolabe* (or mariner's astrolabe) was used to locate stars, the moon, and planets to aid in navigation at sea.

G - Gold - A promise of wealth. Specifically, explorers such as Christopher Columbus were looking for a quicker route to Asian trade markets. Such a route would prevent travel-ing through the Muslim controlled lands of the Middle East.

G - God - The Europeans wanted to spread Christianity.

G - Glory - Explorers wanted their own personal fame and fortune, as did the countries that sponsored the voyages.

During the Age of Exploration, European countries traveled and conquered the Empires of the New World (Native America).

Definition: Line of Demarcation /Treaty of Tordesillas

Spain and Portugal were the two early powers of exploration, and they fought over land in the New World. In 1493, Pope Alexander VI attempted to bring peace. He drew a *line of demarcation* on a map and said that Spain would get everything west of it, and Portugal would get the land to the east. In 1494, the Treaty of Tordesillas moved the line a bit to the west to give Portugal more territory in modern-day Brazil. Today, this is why most people in South America speak Spanish, yet Brazil to the east speaks Portuguese.

Question: What explorers should I know about c1500?

Answer:

1. Christopher Columbus - Italian, but exploring for Spain. He was sent by King Ferdinand and Queen Isabella in 1492 to find a quicker western route to India. Instead, he found Native America.

2. Vasco da Gama - Portuguese. He found a direct sea route to India for spices and other trade.

3. British and Dutch East India Companies - England and the Netherlands set up powerful trading companies in India (explained more in depth later).

4. Ferdinand Magellan - Portuguese. He was the first to circumnavigate (completely sail around) Earth.

Definition: Conquistadors

These were Spanish explorers who looked to *conquer* and liquidate the resources of Native America. Conquistadors to know:

1. Hernando Cortés - He conquered the Aztec Empire and its leader, Montezuma II, in 1521. Though outnumbered, ***use of advanced weapons and gunpowder***, as well as the recruitment of the Aztec's enemies, led the Spanish to victory.

2. Francisco Pizarro - With the use of advanced weapons, he conquered the Incan Empire and their capital of Cuzco, c1533.

Definition: *Encomienda* System

Victories for the Spanish in the New World led to a massive collection of gold and other riches. The Spanish forced Native Americans to help remove such resources in a labor system called ***encomienda***. Though it was supposed to be fair, *encomienda* resembled slavery, as rights were denied to the natives. By 1550, Spain ended this practice.

Definition: Columbian Exchange

One of the greatest examples of cultural diffusion, the Columbian Exchange was the trading of all plants, animals, resources, and diseases between Europe and the Americas. Did you know that in 1491 there were no pumpkins in Europe?

To Europe came peanuts, avocados, turkey, pumpkins, corn, and potatoes.

To the New World came horses, rice, wheat, cows, olives, and diseases such as smallpox and influenza.

The transfer of diseases ultimately depleted Native American populations. African slave-labor became more prevalent in the Americas, as after centuries of European contact, they were immune to such diseases.

Definition: Middle Passage

The Middle Passage was the ***Triangular Trade's*** central journey which brought slaves from Africa to the Caribbean. As for the Triangular Trade, molasses from the Caribbean was brought to New England, distilled into rum, and then traded to African kings for the slaves.

Definition: Mercantilism and Commercial Revolution

Mercantilism is an economic system where the European Mother Country (whether it be Spain, France, Netherlands, or England) extracted raw materials, such as gold or tobacco, from their colonies. They sold finished goods to the colonies as well. The sole purpose of the colonies was to make the Mother Country rich and self-sufficient.

The expansion of international trade and colonization led to new business ventures. This time of opportunity was called the ***Commercial Revolution*** and lasted from the late fifteenth century until the seventeenth century.

Question: What was the social hierarchy of the New World?

Answer: From most powerful to least, you should know:

Peninsulares - People who were born in Spain and could hold the highest offices in the New World.

Creoles - Spanish people who were born in the New World. Along with the Peninsulares, they controlled most of the wealth.

Mestizos - People of Spanish and Native American ancestry.

Mulattos - People of African and European ancestry.

Native Americans - Most numerous, but had the fewest rights.

Mestizos adopted Christianity. Above is a painting of The Last Supper *from Peru. The main course has become guinea pig, a local delicacy.*

Review Questions

1. Desertification has been most concerning in Africa's
   A) Sahel
   B) Savannah
   C) Rain Forest
   D) Steppe

2. The Bantu were most associated with
   A) the Trans-Atlantic Slave Trade
   B) expanding Islam throughout Africa
   C) establishing a gold-salt trade on the east coast of Africa
   D) spreading language through migration

3. Mansa Musa of Mali was instrumental in
   A) spreading Islam throughout his Empire
   B) establishing trade in Eastern Africa
   C) defeating the Mutapa Empire
   D) selling slaves to Europeans as part of the Triangular Trade

4. African Kingdoms of Western Africa c1000 found their greatest profits in the trading of
   A) slaves
   B) gold and salt
   C) pottery
   D) spices

5. Pueblos in the southwest of the modern-day United States were constructed by which culture?
   A) Olmec
   B) Chavin
   C) Zapotec
   D) Anasazi

6. The Aztec and Inca were similar in their
   A) worship of a sun deity
   B) constructions of settlements in the Andes Mountains
   C) ability to defeat European invaders
   D) use of Cuzco as a trading center

7. Terrace farming was a productive method of agricultural harvest. It was achieved by
   A) leveling land on mountains
   B) burning a forest and using the ashes for fertilizer
   C) rotating crops across three fields
   D) leaving land unfarmed for one year

8. *Encomienda* was
   A) an exchange of goods
   B) a technique for sailing a great distance
   C) the middle passage of the Triangular Trade
   D) a system of forced labor

9. Conquistadors were those Spaniards who
   A) brought European crops and goods to the New World
   B) used their technologically advanced weapons to take over New World Empires
   C) refused to use caravel ships for exploration
   D) mined gold in Asia

10. Which of the following was true of the Columbian Exchange?
   A) The Pope ended all exchanges of plants and animals after the Treaty of Tordesillas
   B) The turkey was brought from Europe to the New World
   C) Horses were introduced to Europe in the sixteenth century
   D) Diseases were brought from Europe to the Americas

Answers and Explanations

1. **A**. The Sahel borders the Sahara desert. As desertification takes place, it grows larger in size.

2. **D**. Bantu migrations brought the roots of many languages that are still spoken today south of the Sahara Desert.

3. **A**. Mansa Musa incorporated Islam into his Empire. He personally went on the hajj.

4. **B**. The gold-salt exchange was a valuable trading system that benefited Western Africa.

5. **D**. The Anasazi were known for constructing adobe (clay-bricked) structures known as pueblos.

6. **A**. Worshipping the sun god was an important aspect of both Incan and Aztec culture.

7. **A**. In order to plant crops in the mountainous regions of the Andes, the Inca needed to level off the land in a process known as terrace farming. Terrace farming was used all over the world, notably in Southeast Asia.

8. **D**. *Encomienda* was a system of forced labor used in Native America by the Spanish Conquistadors.

9. **B**. Although Native American Empires were advanced, militarily they were no match for the weapons of the Conquistadors.

10. **D**. The most catastrophic result of the Columbian Exchange was the transfer of European diseases. Because Native Americans were not immune to diseases such as influenza and smallpox, millions died after contact.

The Age of Absolutism and the Enlightenment

For centuries, absolute monarchs ruled Europe. In most cases, individual rights were limited and kings grew stronger. Because the monarch claimed to be a representative of God, few questioned the extent of their power. However, in the seventeenth century a movement in philosophy known as the Enlightenment began. Popular philosophical thought led to a demand for natural rights and liberty. Some monarchs extended rights to their people. Others did not. By the middle of the eighteenth century, demands for freedom grew louder and more violent.

HERE IS WHAT YOU NEED TO KNOW:

• THE AGE OF ABSOLUTISM
Definition: Absolutism

Monarchs (kings and queens) ruled with complete power from c1500-c1740. As seen in ancient China (Mandate of Heaven) and Egypt (theocracy), there was a belief that the king was the representative of God. In Europe, this theory was called ***divine right***.

Definition: Louis (Bourbon) XIV - France

Before Louis took the throne, Cardinal Richelieu governed. A cardinal is a Catholic clergy title. Because Louis XIII was a weak King, Richelieu became his powerful official. Richelieu favored Catholicism in France, and legislated against French Protestants called ***Huguenots***. Huguenots had been given freedoms previously with the 1598 Edict of Nantes.

Louis (Bourbon) XIV was the prototypical absolute ruler c1700. Nicknamed "The Sun King," Louis said ***"I am the state."*** He expanded the ***Palace of Versailles*** into one of the most elaborate compounds in the world. Complete with thousands of rooms, ornate statues, and extensive gardens, this symbol of France was built at the expense of the suffering and starving peasants.

Louis XIV fought many wars during his 72 year reign. Although France became a strong force, weaker countries teamed up against them to keep French territorial gains minimal. During his rule, the debt of the country increased because of his lavish spending.

The famous Hall of Mirrors at Versailles. Endless chandeliers and mirrors were constructed while many in France were starving.

Definition: Philip II of Spain

Gaining much wealth from the riches of the New World, Philip's Spain was the wealthiest nation in Europe c1580. Philip defended Catholicism as Protestantism spread throughout

55

Western Europe. Spain ultimately squandered its fortune and went into economic decline. In 1588, Philip's **Spanish Armada** was defeated by England. In time, the British became the supreme naval force in the world.

Question: What wars plagued Europe from 1618-1763?

Answer: Wars took place on the continent during this time period. Here are three:

1. Thirty Years' War - 1618-1648 - This war began with the **Defenestration of Prague** when Protestants threw three Catholics out of a window (they survived). Thus, the war was caused by religion. However, it evolved into a larger conflict over French and Hapsburg (explained next) dominance on the continent. In the **Peace of Westphalia** that ended the conflict, the Hapsburgs lost territory and France gained some land.

2. War of Spanish Succession - 1701-1714 - This was a battle to see if a French Bourbon (Louis XIV's relative) could take the Spanish throne and unite the Kingdoms. It was agreed that a Bourbon could take the throne, but Spain and France would have to remain separate entities.

3. Seven Years' War - 1756-1763 - Known as the French and Indian War in North America (which began in 1754), this world war saw Britain defeat France to maintain their colonial Empire in the New World and India.

Definition: Hapsburgs

The Hapsburgs were an Empire in Central Europe, notably Austria and Hungary. After the Thirty Years' War their Empire expanded, as they conquered lands once controlled by the Ottoman Empire in the Balkans of Eastern Europe. **Maria Theresa** is the most relevant name to know. A devout Catholic, she was not tolerant of other religions.

The thorn in Maria's side was **Frederick the Great** of **Prussia** (in modern-day Germany). When Maria took the throne, Frederick looked to gain land from her in the **War of the Austrian Succession**. Frederick eventually secured the territory of Silesia in 1748.

Definition: Ivan the Terrible

Ivan IV was a **czar** (Russian king) who restricted the powers of Russian nobles called **boyars**. After his first wife died in 1560, Ivan went on a killing spree, executing thousands of boyars. He then took their land. Ivan also killed his son in a fit of rage. Because his other son was unfit to rule, Russia went through a few decades of czar uncertainty. Eventually it was the **Romanov** family that came to power. The House of Romanov would rule from 1613-1917.

Definition: Peter the Great

Peter Romanov was a czar who wanted to imitate Western Europe, or **westernize** c1680. This meant to modernize Russia militarily, culturally, economically, and technologically. Peter traveled to the west with his army. Examples of westernization were: increasing the size of the army, expanding education, and removing Mongol influence from society in the way people dressed and presented themselves. Because all great nations of the West had impressive capitals, the new city of **St. Petersburg** was constructed in Russia. It was built with serf labor.

Peter the Great also raised the status of women. In addition to easing restrictions on dress, he allowed women to mingle with men at social gatherings. Furthermore, he encouraged greater educational opportunities for women.

Definition: Stuarts of England

After Elizabeth Tudor (Elizabeth I) died with

no heir, the Stuart family ruled England. You need to know:

1. James I - A cousin of Elizabeth, he assumed the throne. During his reign came a new interpretation of the Bible (King James Bible).

2. Charles I - He did not consult Parliament in governing affairs, and ruled absolutely. Charles and his supporters, known as Cavaliers, were defeated by *General Oliver Cromwell* in the *Puritan Revolution/English Civil War* (1642-1649). Charles was brought to trial by the Puritan victors, and was executed for treason. Cromwell ruled as a military dictator until 1658.

3. Charles II - With the people longing for a return of the monarchy, Charles II resumed Stuart rule in 1660. This was called the *Restoration*. During his reign, the *Habeas Corpus Act* was passed by Parliament. It guaranteed the accused a right to go before a judge. One could not just be thrown into prison.

4. James II - He took power in 1685 and favored Catholicism. This upset English Protestants, including his daughter Mary.

5. William and Mary - Aided by her husband, a Dutch prince, Mary overthrew James in the bloodless *Glorious Revolution* of 1688.

Definition: Constitutional/Limited Monarchy

Under the rule of William and Mary, the absolute monarchy ceased to exist. Instead, a new *limited,* or *constitutional, monarchy* prevailed with Parliament having immense strength in the creation of laws. Parliament drafted the Bill of Rights in 1689 to ensure freedom of speech, fair taxation, and other personal liberties. To recap, the three documents that limited the monarchy over the years were:

1. Magna Carta - 1215 - The Great Charter was forced upon King John to sign. This document limited the king's power and gave rights to the people.

2. Habeas Corpus Act - 1679 - Guaranteed the accused the right to go before a judge.

3. Bill of Rights - 1689

• THE ENLIGHTENMENT
Definition: Scientific Revolution c1550-1700

The Enlightenment was mostly a political movement, but it coincided with new discoveries in science. Philosophers such as Francis Bacon and René Descartes attacked the scientific conclusions made by Aristotle. Descartes relied on math and reason to prove his theories. This use of observation developed into the *Scientific Method*. The Scientific Method was a new sequence of investigation that was used to test a hypothesis through experimentation. After logical steps were taken, a conclusion could be derived.

What you should also know about the Scientific Revolution:

1. *Heliocentric model* - This was Nicolaus Copernicus' belief that the planets revolved around the sun. This idea contrasted with the geocentric model that declared the Earth as the center of the universe.

2. *Galileo Galilei* - He was a scientist who discovered that objects of different weights fall at the same speed (this went against Aristotle's theory). He also observed the moons of Jupiter and confirmed Copernicus' theories. His findings upset the Church, and at trial he was forced to retract his observations. Despite his retraction, Galileo spent his remaining days under house arrest.

3. Andreas Vesalius - Gave new ideas on anatomy and how to perform surgery.

4. Isaac Newton - Researched universal gravitation and created three laws of motion.

Definition: Enlightenment/Age of Reason of the Eighteenth Century

Coinciding with the Scientific Revolution was the Enlightenment. This Age of Reason was a movement, mostly in the eighteenth century, that looked to reform (progressively change) society through knowledge and reason. A goal of most Enlightenment thinkers was to protect natural rights.

Question: Which Enlightenment writers should I know?

Answer: Enlightenment philosophers used reason to define the liberties they thought people should have in nature. You should know:

1. Thomas Hobbes (English) - *Leviathan*, 1651 - He believed that people created government, calling this notion a "social contract." A Leviathan is a monster, and a metaphor for government. Like Machiavelli before him, Hobbes believed that people are greedy and need to be kept in check by a strong and absolute ruler. Despite his support for monarchy, Hobbes is included in the Enlightenment. Generally, the following three philosophers are more relevant to know.

2. John Locke (English) - **Two Treatises of Government**, 1689 - He believed that people were born free with natural rights such as life, liberty, and property. His ideas were adopted by Thomas Jefferson in the American Declaration of Independence.

3. Jean-Jacques Rousseau (French) - *Social Contract*, 1762 - He said that government should rule for the common good. A famous quote of his was that, "Man is born free, and everywhere he is in chains." Here, Rousseau was describing unjust laws which prevent natural rights and liberty.

4. Baron de Montesquieu (French) - *The Spirit of the Laws*, 1748 - He illustrated the concept of **separation of powers**, where the legislative branch (makes laws), executive branch (enforces laws) and judicial branch (interprets laws) controlled the government. All three would operate under a system of **checks and balances** that would prevent one branch from getting too strong. Separation of powers was adopted by numerous nations, including the United States.

5. Voltaire (French) - In the eighteenth century he wrote hundreds of essays regarding the themes of freedom of speech, religion, and other social reforms. He was a supporter of separation of church and state.

Definition: Mary Wollstonecraft

In 1792, this British activist published *A Vindication of the Rights of Woman*. She argued that women should receive an equal education to men, and should participate in politics and the economy outside of the home. Still, it would be decades before women received equality in Europe.

Definition: *Encyclopédie*

c1760, Denis Diderot was an editor for this publication in France that printed many essays. The essays supported Enlightenment ideas and looked to change the way people viewed government.

Question: How did the Enlightenment impact the arts in Europe?

Answer:

1. Classical music began to thrive in Central Europe under the likes of Wolfgang Amadeus Mozart (*The Magic Flute*), and later Ludwig van Beethoven (renowned for his symphonies).

2. In the Age of Absolutism, many castles displayed **baroque** architecture. This was a colorful and lavish style. In the late 1700s, a less elaborate movement called **neoclassical** emerged. This was inspired by the architecture of Western Civilization (Greece, Rome, and the Renaissance). Another movement in

Ornate baroque statue at the Palace of Versailles

France, called rococo (or late baroque), also went against the ornate style of baroque.

3. **Romanticism** was a movement in art, music, literature, and even architecture that evolved in the late eighteenth century. It emphasized spontaneous emotions and heroism, and was a reaction to the rational balance of the Classical Period. By the nineteenth century, the harsh working conditions of the Industrial Revolution made people want stories they could relate to. This led to a rise in **realism**, or entertainment that reflected what was really going on in society.

4. In the nineteenth century, French artists such as Edouard Manet, Edgar Degas, and Claude Monet froze their impressions of a moment in time. This art movement is called **impressionism**. Some artists, such as Dutch painter Vincent van Gogh, concentrated more on emotions. These artists are known as post-impressionists.

Definition: Enlightened Despots

A despot is another term for an absolute ruler. Enlightened despots were those who supported the Age of Reason. Rulers such as Frederick the Great of Prussia and Catherine the Great of Russia supported modernization. They embraced the arts, education, religious toleration, and an end to certain torture punishments.

Review Questions

1. Which was true of France's economy under Louis XIV?

   A) A new fair code of taxation was passed to aid the peasants

   B) The debt of the country greatly increased during his reign

   C) Industrialization began in the first decade of his rule

   D) There was vast economic prosperity for all classes

2. Peter the Great wanted Russia to

   A) isolate itself from the rest of the world

   B) trade only with countries in the East

   C) imitate the nations of Western Europe

   D) abolish serfdom in the Empire

3. Divine right is most accurately defined as the

   A) seizing of noble lands by a king

   B) centralization of power within a two-house legislature

   C) protections given to property and free speech

   D) belief that the monarch is a representative of God

4. All of the following were influential in limiting the monarchy of England from 1215-1689 EXCEPT:

   A) Habeas Corpus Act

   B) Bill of Rights

   C) The Restoration

   D) Magna Carta

5. Religion and the Peace of Westphalia were associated with which war?

   A) Thirty Years' War

   B) War of Spanish Succession

   C) War of the Austrian Succession

   D) Seven Years' War

6. Which of the following best describes the heliocentric model?

   A) The Earth and planets revolve around the sun

   B) A body in motion stays in motion

   C) The Earth is at the center of the universe

   D) Planets and the sun all revolve around Earth

7. The laws of gravity are attributed to which scientist?

   A) Isaac Newton

   B) Andreas Vesalius

   C) Nicolaus Copernicus

   D) René Descartes

8. Belief in life, liberty, and property are most associated with the writings of

   A) Jean-Jacques Rousseau

   B) John Locke

   C) Voltaire

   D) Baron de Montesquieu

9. In *The Spirit of the Laws*, Baron de Montesquieu advocated for

A) speech rights
B) separation of powers
C) property qualifications to vote
D) freedom of religion

10. Enlightened despots were those monarchs who

A) censored all philosophers who promoted democracy
B) wanted to limit educational opportunities
C) were open to some of the ideas brought forth by philosophers
D) looked to extend their Empires overseas

Answers and Explanations

1. **B**. Louis spent money lavishly during his reign. Most notably, he renovated the elaborate Palace of Versailles. His spending left France in debt.

2. **C**. Peter wanted to imitate Western Europe and modernize Russia.

3. **D**. Similar to a theocracy in Egypt, or Chinese Mandate of Heaven, divine right meant that the absolute monarch of Europe was a representative of God.

4. **C**. The Restoration of 1660 meant a return to monarchy in England. Charles II did not rule as absolutely as his father Charles I. Parliament passed the Habeas Corpus Act during his reign, which extended rights to the accused.

5. **A**. Although the Thirty Years' War escalated into a larger conflict, it began as a religious war.

6. **A**. Nicolaus Copernicus' model stated that the Earth and the other planets revolve around the sun.

7. **A**. Isaac Newton was best known for his laws of motion and universal gravitation.

8. **B**. These were John Locke's ideas that helped inspire the American Declaration of Independence. Locke's *Two Treatises of Government* was his most famous work.

9. **B**. Montesquieu favored a government with three branches (Legislative, Executive, Judicial) where a system of checks and balances kept each branch from becoming too powerful.

10. **C**. Enlightened despots, such as Catherine the Great and Frederick the Great, were open to some of the ideas set forth by Enlightenment thinkers.

The French Revolution and Napoleon

Enlightenment thought was one of the major inspirations behind the bloody revolution that consumed France in the late 1700s. By 1789, France was controlled by a regime that did not fairly represent most of the population. Swiftly, the people revolted and established a Republic in France. However, what was in name a Republic was really a radical government that looked to eliminate all opposition. After a Reign of Terror bled France, Napoleon Bonaparte took over the country and ruled as a military dictator. Napoleon's thirst for an Empire eventually led to his downfall, as overexpansion and war losses led twice to his exile.

HERE IS WHAT YOU NEED TO KNOW:
Question: What were the main causes of the French Revolution?

Answer: Mnemonic Device: **MEAT**

M - Monarchy. The rule of King Louis XVI and Queen Marie Antoinette was inefficient and did not meet the needs of the people.

E - Enlightenment. Ideas of liberty and equality made citizens further resent the absolute monarchy of France.

A - American Revolution. The King and Queen spent a lot of money to help America defeat the British. All the while, people were starving in France. In addition, there was a belief that if the Americans could be successful in a revolution that brought liberty, so too could the French.

T - Taxes/**T**hird Estate. The Third Estate made up about 98% of the people. Despite not having most of the wealth in France, they paid more than their fair share in taxes. They also had little say in government.

Definition: Old Regime/Three Estates

The Old Regime was the historic class and

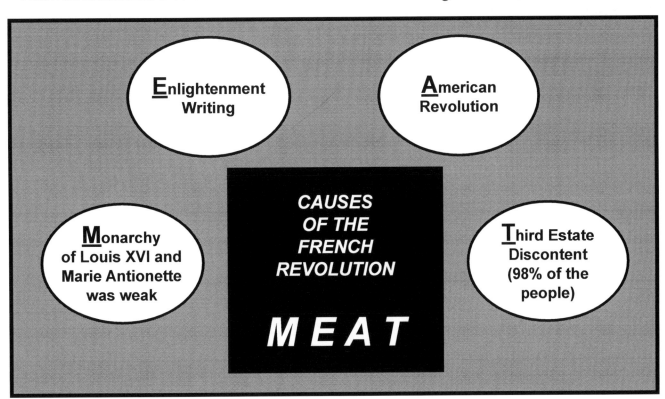

Enlightenment Writing

American Revolution

Monarchy of Louis XVI and Marie Antionette was weak

CAUSES OF THE FRENCH REVOLUTION

MEAT

Third Estate Discontent (98% of the people)

political structure of France. From most powerful to least, it included:

The First Estate - Clergy, who owned a great deal of land.

The Second Estate - Nobles, who also controlled a great amount of wealth.

The Third Estate - The Third Estate was divided into the bourgeoisie (explained below) and the peasants. Peasants made up most of this Estate.

Definition: Bourgeoisie

A branch of the Third Estate was the bourgeoisie. They were well-educated artisans and capitalists who familiarized themselves with Enlightenment thought. The bourgeoisie believed they were entitled a say in government because of their education and standing in society.

Definition: National Assembly, June 17, 1789

France was spending more money than it had. When Louis XVI asked the Estates General (representatives from the three Estates) for more tax revenue, the Third Estate became enraged for multiple reasons. Though comprised of 98% of the people, they had the same amount of representatives as the other two Estates. To make matters worse, each Estate only had one vote. This meant that the First and Second Estates could always outvote the Third Estate. Enraged by the structure, and inspired by Enlightenment ideas, the Third Estate declared itself the *National Assembly* of France that could pass laws for the people.

Definition: Tennis Court Oath, June 20, 1789

Locked out of an Estates General meeting, National Assembly (Third Estate) members broke into an indoor tennis court. There, they took an oath to make a new constitution for France.

Definition: Storming of the Bastille, July 14, 1789

A symbol of absolutism in France, the Bastille was a prison that housed political criminals. Although King Louis XVI began to listen to the demands of the people, he also called in neutral (Swiss) troops to protect France from mob rule. Nonetheless a crowd overtook the Bastille. This event triggered the first bloodshed of the Revolution, which today is celebrated in France as Bastille Day.

In the aftermath of the Bastille there were riots and mob chaos. Fueled by rumors that both the King and the first two Estates were going to imprison or kill peasants, hysteria unfolded known as the *Great Fear*. Peasants armed themselves with whatever they could and paraded through the streets. Many looted the homes of nobles.

Question: What other events from the French Revolution should I know?

Answer:

1. Women in Paris took to the streets to protest the inflation of bread prices. They broke into the Palace of Versailles (just outside of Paris), and demanded that the King and Queen rule from Paris. In 1791, the royal family attempted to escape to Austria, but was recognized near the French border and captured.

2. The National Assembly finished the constitution (as pledged on the tennis court). After Louis' blessing, lawmaking power was given to a new *Legislative Assembly*.

3. Austria, which was loyal to Louis, demanded that he be restored to power. The Legislative Assembly declared war on Austria in 1792, and lost many early battles. Austria never did conquer Paris though, and the Legislative Assembly, and later a newly elected *National Convention*, maintained power.

4. In 1793, a powerless Louis was put on tri-

al and found guilty of treason. He was executed via the *guillotine* (device used to chop off heads). The Queen was executed months later.

Definition: *Declaration of the Rights of Man and of the Citizen*, 1789

This was a document, similar to the American Declaration of Independence, that declared all men to be created equal. It promised to protect the natural rights of individuals. The words had far reaching implications, as they would inspire revolution as far away as Latin America. In France, the demands for *liberty, equality, and fraternity* could be heard throughout the countryside.

However, women were not included. *Olympe de Gouges* spoke out for female equality. She was unsuccessful in her campaign, and was executed during the Reign of Terror (explained later).

Definition: Political Spectrum: Radicals, Moderates, and Conservatives

In the Legislative Assembly, there were:

Radicals (who sat on the left) - They represented people such as the *sans-culottes*, or those laborers and merchants who wanted to totally change the way France conducted its government.

Conservatives (who sat on the right) - They were fine with having a limited monarch. Many of them were aristocratic émigrés, or royal supporters who emigrated from France during the violence.

Moderates (who sat in the middle) - They were still undecided on the role of the monarchy in France.

Related, you should know the *political spectrum*, or the explanation of ideologies in politics. To generalize, those who favor more reform for individual liberties are called *liberals*. Those who want little or no reform are *conservatives*. The *moderates* can lean either

way. *Revolutionaries* are radicals who want much more change than legally possible. *Reactionaries* wish to "turn back the clock" on society. In the case of the French Revolution, reactionaries would be those looking to restore the absolute monarchy.

Definition: Jacobins

The Jacobins were a revolutionary political club that wanted to eliminate all aspects of monarchy and make France a Republic. The Jacobins turned to violence to achieve their goals. Their leaders were Jean-Paul Marat, Georges Danton, and Maximilien Robespierre.

Definition: Maximilien Robespierre and the Reign of Terror

Robespierre seized power. He wanted to rid France of people who supported nobility and the monarchy. To do this, he established the *Committee of Public Safety* to sniff out enemies of the Republic. Between 1793 and 1794, thousands of so-called traitors were executed in what would be known as the *Reign of Terror*. Even Danton, a once loyal Jacobin, was executed. Marat was stabbed to death in a bathtub by a female political opponent named Charlotte Corday.

Definition: The Directory

Robespierre's killing-spree was too much to endure for the French people. Robespierre was guillotined in 1794. In the aftermath of the terror, a moderate five-member executive branch known as the *Directory* took over alongside a two-house legislature. The Directory appointed *Napoleon Bonaparte* to lead France's army.

Definition: Coup d'état, 1799

Napoleon Bonaparte's popularity as a General was growing. When the French Directory was internally falling apart, Napoleon pounced on the government. He suddenly seized power in 1799. Such a "blow of state" is called a *coup d'état*.

Question: Under Napoleon, what parts of Europe did France control?

Answer: Napoleon had a foot in just about every country in Europe. His great victory at *Austerlitz* in 1805 was enough to defeat the *Third Coalition* (European nations who banded together to fight France). The Napoleonic Wars were fought from 1803-1815. At his peak:

1. Napoleon controlled modern-day France, Belgium, Netherlands, Spain, Italy, and Poland.

2. Austria, Prussia, Denmark, and Russia were allies through treaties.

France gave up much of its New World territory, as a slave uprising by Toussaint L'Ouverture in Haiti made it difficult to control the sugar crop. A great deal of land in the New World was sold to the United States in the Louisiana Purchase of 1803.

Definition: Battle of Trafalgar, 1805

This was a naval battle that Napoleon lost to British commander Horatio Nelson off the coast of Spain. The defeat was one of Napoleon's unsuccessful attempts to conquer the island nation of Great Britain.

Definition: Napoleonic Code

Napoleon crowned himself Emperor in 1804. He placed the crown on his own head rather than have the Pope do it for him. To legislate for the Empire, a legal code was named for him. Although the code gave equal rights to all men under the law, it limited freedom of speech. Furthermore, women's rights were decreased and male dominance was proclaimed.

Question: What were Napoleon's three mistakes?

Answer: **CPR**

1. **C - *Continental System***. Despite conquering much of Europe, Napoleon never defeated Britain. Geographically, Britain is an island. Beginning in 1806, Napoleon hoped to blockade, or surround Britain with ships, to prevent all trade. This was a failure because Britain's navy was strong enough to resist, and other European nations did not like being told whom they could trade with. Many illegally traded with Great Britain anyway.

2. **P - *Peninsular War***, 1808-1814. Napoleon controlled Spain, but wanted Portugal. He marched his soldiers through the Iberian (Spain and Portugal) Peninsula and attacked. Napoleon lost about 300,000 soldiers in this war, and never took over Portugal.

3. **R - *Invasion of Russia***, 1812. He invaded his former ally, Russia. When Napoleon got deep enough into the country, Czar Alexander I ordered the land to be burned (called scorched-earth policy). This destruction of agriculture left Napoleon's army to starve through the harsh Russian winter. He lost almost his entire force of half a million soldiers during the campaign.

Definition: Elba and Hundred Days

After his defeat in Russia, Napoleon was banished to the island of *Elba* near Italy. Not guarded too tightly, he escaped in 1815 and marched through France's countryside to gather supporters. He attempted to regain his Empire for about one hundred days. This attempt ended on June 18, 1815 when he lost the *Battle of Waterloo*. Napoleon was banished to the island of *Saint Helena* in the Atlantic. There, he died in 1821.

Definition: Congress of Vienna

This was a meeting in Austria from 1814-1815. Led by Austrian Prince *Klemens von*

Metternich, diplomats embraced ideas such as establishing a *balance of power* in Europe and restoring the *legitimacy* of the monarchs dethroned by Napoleon.

Fearful of revolutions similar to the one seen in France, coalitions such as the *Holy Alliance* and Metternich's *Concert of Europe* were formed. It was agreed that if an uprising broke out in one country, the members of the alliances would put it down. These alliances did not prevent the wars to come in the nineteenth century.

Question: How did South American countries get their independence from European nations?

Answer: Inspired by the French Revolution and the Enlightenment, Latin America saw revolutions c1820 led by:

1. Simón Bolívar - Known as the *Liberator*, he helped bring self-rule to much of South America including Colombia, Bolivia, Peru, and Venezuela.

2. José San Martin - He fought alongside Bolívar, and helped free Chile, Peru, and Argentina.

3. Toussaint L'Ouverture - As mentioned above, in 1801 he led an uprising of slaves in Haiti that eventually led to its independence from France in 1804.

4. Mexico also declared independence in 1821. With the help of Miguel Hidalgo and José Morelos, Mexico received independence from Spain after bloody conflict. In the middle of the nineteenth century, Mexican politician **Benito Juárez** presented liberal reforms in a movement called La Reforma. He advocated for separation of church and state, and increased education for the poor.

5. In contrast, Brazil received its independence from Portugal in 1822 through mostly peaceful measures. However, Portugal did not recognize their independence until 1825.

Review Questions

1. All of the following were causes of the French Revolution EXCEPT:

A) A lack of government representation for the Third Estate

B) Enlightenment philosophy

C) The appointment of Napoleon Bonaparte to command the military

D) Inspiration from the American Revolution

2. The violent spark of the French Revolution began on July 14, 1789 at the

A) Bastille

B) signing of the Tennis Court Oath

C) Palace of Versailles

D) Cathedral of Notre Dame

3. The bourgeoisie was mainly represented by

A) nobles who supported the king

B) clergy members of the first estate

C) educated merchants and artisans

D) the poorest class of peasants

4. The Jacobins and King Louis XVI both would agree with

A) dividing all noble lands amongst the people

B) imprisoning or executing opponents of their policies

C) ridding the country of organized religion

D) accepting rule through divine right

5. Which of the following never became a part of Napoleon's Empire?

A) Spain

B) Italy

C) Netherlands

D) Great Britain

6. Napoleon's final defeat in the Hundred Days occurred as a result of which battle?

A) Moscow

B) Waterloo

C) Elba

D) Trafalgar

7. Historians consider all of the following to contribute to Napoleon's downfall EXCEPT:

A) Peninsular War

B) Invasion of Russia

C) Battle of Austerlitz

D) Continental System

8. An outcome of the Congress of Vienna was

A) restoration of the monarchs dethroned by Napoleon

B) the handing over of the French government to the Legislative Assembly

C) execution of King Louis XVI

D) the ratification of a French constitution

9. The *Declaration of the Rights of Man* inspired which of the following?

A) Napoleon's coup d'état

B) The Congress of Vienna

C) Latin American independence movements

D) The American Revolution

10. Who of the following led a slave revolt against the French?

A) José San Martin

B) Simón Bolívar

C) Benito Juárez

D) Toussaint L'Ouverture

Answers and Explanations

1. **C**. Napoleon took command of the military in a coup d'état years after the Revolution began.

2. **A**. The Bastille was a prison, and a symbol of the King of France.

3. **C**. Many of the revolutionaries of France were part of the bourgeoisie of the Third Estate. They were well educated and usually accumulated some degree of wealth.

4. **B**. Although the Jacobins were against the King, they used some of the monarch's methods to intimidate opponents of the Revolution. During the Reign of Terror thousands were executed under Maximilien Robespierre.

5. **D**. Napoleon attempted to harm Britain through battle and trade embargoes. Britain never became part of Napoleon's Empire.

6. **B**. Waterloo, in Belgium, was the scene of Napoleon's final defeat. He was exiled to the island of St. Helena shortly thereafter.

7. **C**. The Battle of Austerlitz in Central Europe was one of Napoleon's greatest victories. There, he defeated a group of European nations known as the Third Coalition.

8. **A**. The Congress of Vienna "turned back the clock" on Europe, and under the leadership of Prince Klemens von Metternich, former monarchs dethroned by Napoleon were restored to power.

9. **C**. The ideas of the French Revolution spread to Latin America. Led by Simón Bolívar, and others, South American nations began to declare their independence from European powers.

10. **D**. Toussaint led a slave revolt in Haiti. By 1804, Haiti received its independence. At about the same time of the revolt, Napoleon sold the Louisiana Territory to the United States.

Nationalism, the Industrial Revolution, and Nineteenth Century Western Europe

A wave of nationalism swept over Europe in the middle of the nineteenth century, as revolution and war led to the formation of new nation-states. As this was occurring, an Industrial Revolution was taking place in Britain and spreading to the rest of the world. Goods were being produced by machines in factories. In addition, new methods of transportation led to urbanization. However not everyone was thrilled with capitalism, as socialist writers encouraged the working class to fight for more rights. Regarding rights at this time, citizens within Great Britain and its colonies received more liberties during the nineteenth century.

HERE IS WHAT YOU NEED TO KNOW:

• NATIONALISM
Definition: Nationalism

Nationalism is a belief that one's loyalty rests with the people of a nation-state because of a common culture, heritage, set of beliefs, or interest. Typically, nationalism is accompanied by strong pride for one's nation-state/country.

In the bloody year of *1848*, revolutions broke out all over Europe as nationalism and dissatisfaction with governments ran wild. France, and modern-day Germany and Italy, were greatly affected. People wanted more democracy, individual liberties, and improvements to working conditions.

Definition: Italian Unification, 1848-1870

Italy was not a country until *Camillo di Cavour* of Sardinia linked up with northern Italy, and *Giuseppe Garibaldi's* army of Redshirts marched through Southern Italy. They helped unify the entire boot (Italy is shaped like a boot). The Pope provided the large area containing Rome known as the *Papal States*. The Church kept a small piece of land which is called Vatican City.

Definition: German Unification, 1848-1871

As stated earlier, nationalistic revolutions tore through modern-day Germany in 1848. In 1862, Otto von Bismarck became prime minister of *Prussia*, which would evolve into Germany. Bismarck unified Germany with *"Blood and Iron,"* as through war, Prussia won land. Bismarck used the diplomacy of *realpolitik*. This meant ruling with authority for practical, realistic, and material reasons…not for idealistic or moral ones.

In a short Seven Weeks' War, Prussia took land from Austria. In the Franco-Prussian War of 1870-71, they received the territories of *Alsace and Lorraine* from France. King Wilhelm I of Prussia declared himself *kaiser*, or the first German Emperor. Thus formed the *Second Reich* (Holy Roman Empire being the first one, and Adolf Hitler would become the Third Reich).

• THE INDUSTRIAL REVOLUTION
Definition: Industrial Revolution

During the second half of the eighteenth century, there was an enormous increase in the number of machine-made finished goods being produced in factories across England. Such ideas of industrialization spread to mainland Europe, the United States, and eventually the world. Because factories offered jobs, people migrated to cities in a process called *urbanization*.

Urbanization was enhanced by railroads that linked rural and urban (city) areas. Steam-powered vehicles, such as Robert Fulton's steamboat, were available because of James Watt's fuel-efficient steam engine. Urbanization had its share of problems, as pollution, child labor, and unsanitary living conditions were common in cities.

Definition: Agricultural Revolution

Farming techniques improved shortly before the Industrial Revolution. In order to have successful industrial output, an abundance of food would be needed for workers and the people of Europe. Some of the new techniques used were:

1. Crop Rotation - Similar to the Three Field System of the Middle Ages, this technique was used by farmers to ensure good harvests. It was learned that some crops would grow better in the soil if they were planted in the same spots where specific crops bloomed the year before.

2. Enclosures - A fancy word for fences, enclosures were used to create larger farms.

3. Seed Drill - Invented by Jethro Tull, this invention planted seeds evenly in rows, instead of randomly scattering them.

Question: Where did the Industrial Revolution begin c1750?

Answer: England. England, though an island, has abundant natural resources such as coal and hydroelectric (water) power. Resources used to produce finished goods are called *factors of production*. These factors include capital, laborers, land/natural resources, and *entrepreneurship* (explained later). In addition, because it's an island on the English Channel, there are ample harbors suitable for trade. England also has rivers for domestic travel.

Question: What were some of the early inventions of the textile industry in England?

Answer: England's textile factories dominated industry. You should know these eighteenth century inventions:

1. John Kay's *flying shuttle* doubled the speed at which yarn could be spun.

2. James Hargreaves' *spinning jenny* could spin yarn on eight spindles at a time.

3. Samuel Crompton's *spinning mule* spun with the help of hydroelectric (water) power.

Eli Whitney's invention of the cotton gin in the United States helped provide the raw material of cotton for English textile production. Whitney also invented the system of *interchangeable parts*. This meant that if a part of a firearm broke, you could just replace that part…instead of the entire weapon.

Definition: Adam Smith and Capitalism

In 1776 Adam Smith wrote **The Wealth of Nations** where he argued that the government should take its **hands off** the economy and permit a free market. This non-interference concept is called **laissez-faire**.

In the economic system of **capitalism**, business ventures are controlled by private owners who have an incentive to gain from their investments. There is **free-enterprise**, or private ownership of businesses. One who takes the financial risk of operating a business is called an *entrepreneur*. Corporations were also formed. They could issue stock to outside investors looking to own a share of the company.

Definition: Karl Marx and Socialism

During the Industrial Revolution, people were suffering from hard work and an increasing gap between the rich and the poor. Germans Karl Marx and Friedrich Engels wrote **The Communist Manifesto** in 1848 to criticize these situations. They encouraged the lower class, the *proletariat*, to rise up and eliminate all distinctions of classes. Marx favored a **classless society**. In a classless society, there would be *socialism*, where the means of production can be shared by the people. This is the opposite of capitalism, which has individuals striving for the incentive of profit. In an equal socialist state, such incentive would not exist. In an economic, political, and social sense, extreme socialism would be defined by Marx as communism (explained more in depth later).

Luddites were those who protested the massive changes brought forth by the Industrial Revolution. Luddites were upset that machines were replacing skilled laborers.

Definition: Unions

As the Industrial Revolution spread, so did unionization. Still prevalent today, unions are organizations that look to provide protection against the exploitation of the working class. They aim for higher wages and better working conditions. When demands aren't met, unions can go on *strike*, or stop working.

Definition: Jeremy Bentham/John Stuart Mill

These men believed in "the greatest happiness principle" where the government should provide the greatest good for the greatest number. This notion of the morality of actions being judged by their consequences is called *utilitarianism*. In other words, a government's actions would be deemed good if they provided for the happiness of many.

• NINETEENTH CENTURY WESTERN EUROPE

Question: What were some domestic reforms in Great Britain during the reign of Queen Victoria?

Answer: Queen Victoria was known for spreading democracy to the people. During her reign there was a working class *Chartist Movement* which demanded more rights, such as suffrage (voting privileges) for men.

During her reign, Parliament's House of Commons (which was elected unlike the House of Lords) gained much power. The Queen became mostly a figurehead, or ceremonial leader.

Question: In which of its colonies did Great Britain allow self-rule?

Answer: Self-rule meant that Britain would allow certain colonies to govern themselves, despite still being controlled by the British Empire. You should know:

1. Canada became a *dominion* in 1867, meaning it could self-govern.

2. Australia was founded as a *penal colony* for convicted criminals. After persecuting the local Aborigines, the British settled Australia, as well as neighboring New Zealand. In the early 1900s, both became dominions like Canada.

3. Ireland received *home rule* much later. The *potato famine of the middle 1840s* caused a rift between Ireland and Great Britain, as the British did little to help the starving people of Ireland. Over one million people died during the famine. Ireland protested for home rule for decades. In 1921, Southern Ireland received it after a War for Independence. The country formally became the Republic of Ireland in 1949.

It is important to note that Northern Ireland remains part of the United Kingdom. Ireland (Catholic) and Northern Ireland (Protestant) experienced much violence and conflict in the decades following independence. Religious strife still exists today.

Definition: Charles Darwin's Theory of Evolution

First published in 1859, Darwin wrote *On the Origin of Species*. He preached "survival of the fittest," and that species who don't adapt, die. He stated that all species, including human beings, gradually evolve after many years. Darwin made many of his observations at the Galapagos Islands off the west coast of South America. His Theory of Evolution was very controversial because it went against the creation teachings of the Bible.

Theories of Darwin were used to justify European imperialist policies of the nineteenth century (Social Darwinism explained in next chapter). Darwin's ideas still cause some controversy today.

Definition: Dreyfus Affair

France operated under what was called the ***Third Republic*** during the late 1800s. It was an unstable representative democracy. Captain Alfred Dreyfus was a Jewish military officer who was accused of selling secrets to the Germans. He was convicted in 1894 on bad evidence and sentenced to life in prison. It was later proven that other officers set him up for conviction. Dreyfus was ultimately found innocent of the charges, and allowed to return to the military. The case was an example of ***Anti-Semitism***, or prejudice against Jews.

Review Questions

1. Nationalism is most likely to develop in regions that have
   A) isolated city-states
   B) diverse religious practices
   C) vast trade networks that accumulate wealth
   D) people who share a common culture or history

2. German unification in the nineteenth century was accomplished mostly through
   A) peaceful negotiations with France and Poland
   B) treaties and land purchases through Switzerland
   C) war with neighboring countries
   D) negotiations with the Church for the Papal States

3. Why did the Industrial Revolution begin in England in the eighteenth century?
   A) England's vast overseas Asian Empire gave it the raw materials necessary to industrialize
   B) The geography of England provided rich resources and water transportation needed for industrialization
   C) Napoleon's Continental System forced England to become self-sufficient
   D) Because of failed farming techniques, British people looked for other avenues to achieve economic success

4. Luddites and Socialists were similar in that both
   A) believed in laissez-faire economics
   B) wanted free enterprise and entrepreneurialism
   C) resented the Industrial Revolution's impact on society
   D) supported the election of wealthy business owners to Parliament

5. What was the greatest influence on urbanization in Britain c1800?
   A) Readily available jobs in factories
   B) Crop failures in rural areas
   C) Universal male suffrage
   D) International trading opportunities

6. Which inventor's creation led to an increase in crop harvests?
   A) Samuel Crompton
   B) James Watt
   C) John Kay
   D) Jethro Tull

7. Karl Marx and Friedrich Engels would most likely support
   A) a classless society where the workers share the factors of production
   B) laissez-faire capitalism as advocated by Adam Smith
   C) survival of the fittest in business, and educational opportunities for the elite
   D) elimination of labor unions as a means to bargain wages

8. Queen Victoria's reign in Britain in the nineteenth century was known for

A) limiting suffrage rights and the number of elected officials

B) decreasing the legislating power of the House of Commons

C) restoring absolute monarchy, and decreasing the power of Parliament

D) increasing democracy, and limiting the role of the monarch

9. By the twentieth century, self-rule from the British Empire was accomplished in all of the following places EXCEPT:

A) Ireland

B) Australia

C) Canada

D) New Zealand

10. Charles Darwin's research was controversial mostly because

A) he did not take into account issues of natural selection

B) his discoveries went against the basic teachings of the Church

C) he did not acknowledge advanced human intelligence

D) humans never lived in the Galapagos Islands

Answers and Explanations

1. **D**. Nationalism is one of the most important terms of the course. It involves strong pride in one's nation, and develops because of a common culture, history, language, or set of beliefs.

2. **C**. Otto von Bismarck helped unify Germany through "Blood and Iron." This strategy was accompanied by war.

3. **B**. Geographically, England was the perfect spot for the Industrial Revolution because of an abundance of natural resources and water travel.

4. **C**. Not everyone was happy during the Industrial Revolution. Socialism was supported by workers looking to gain more rights. Luddites opposed the mechanization of industry because machines replaced skilled workers.

5. **A**. People moved to cities (urbanized) because jobs were readily available. Similar urbanization took place all over Europe and the United States.

6. **D**. Jethro Tull's seed drill helped plant seeds in even rows deep within the soil.

7. **A**. If all classes were eliminated, true equality would occur. In the *Communist Manifesto*, Marx and Engels advocated for a classless society.

8. **D**. Gradually over centuries, monarchs lost absolute power in Great Britain. Queen Victoria continued this trend by giving more authority to Parliament in the nineteenth century.

9. **A**. For decades, the Irish pushed for home rule. World War I postponed their independence, and it wouldn't be until after the war that the Irish successfully fought for it.

10. **B**. Darwin's theories still remain controversial today because his conclusions dispute the creation teachings of the Bible.

Imperialism and World War I

Nationalism helped fuel the Age of Imperialism of the nineteenth century where nations took over territories for political and economic gain. Socially, the culture of the conqueror was often enforced as well. Around the globe, Western nations competed for the raw materials and markets that weaker territories had to offer. The riches most sought after were in Africa and Asia. Imperialism was one of the causes for World War I, where fighting on the Western and Eastern fronts left millions of soldiers and civilians dead by 1918. After the war, Germany was held accountable by the Treaty of Versailles.

HERE IS WHAT YOU NEED TO KNOW:

• IMPERIALISM
Definition: Imperialism

Imperialism is when one powerful nation takes over a weaker territory and enforces their political, economic, and social ideals onto the conquered. Typically, this was rationalized through **Social Darwinism**, or a belief in "survival of the fittest." Many European nations imperialized in the middle to late nineteenth century. Britain amassed the greatest Empire. Their main focus was Africa and Asia.

Question: Why did nations imperialize?
Answer: **MGM**

1. **M** - **M**oney - To capitalize on rich resources such as gold, jewels, and ivory.

2. **G** - **G**od - To convert to Christianity those seen as "savages." **Rudyard Kipling** wrote the poem, **The White Man's Burden** which spoke of imperialists civilizing inferior races and savages. **Assimilation** is the process whereby the conquered adopts the imperializing nation's culture.

3. **M** - **M**arket - Heavily populated countries were ideal markets for selling finished goods. China and India were the most populous imperialistic markets.

Another G you could use is *geopolitics*. This means to take over locations around the globe for strategic purposes. Islands, for example, could be used as army bases.

Definition: Berlin Conference, 1884-85

European nations assembled in Berlin, Germany to divide up the lands of Africa. Of course, no African leaders were present to object to this division. Britain and France came away with the most territory after the conference. In Africa, Liberia maintained independence. Ethiopia, under Menelik II, pushed back the Italian military to also remain independent.

Definition: Boer Wars, 1880-81, 1899-1902

South Africa was thriving under the Zulu chief **Shaka** c1800. However, years later the Boers (Dutch settlers) took over the region. When diamonds and other riches were discovered there, the British swooped in. Two wars were fought, the first from 1880-81, and the second from 1899-1902. The British used concentration camps against the Boers which upset other European nations. The British won, and the Union of South Africa remained in their hands until 1961.

Definition: Crimean War, 1854-1856

The Russians also hoped to gain land, as the Ottoman Empire was falling apart by 1854. Britain and France helped push back Russian advances. Note: This was the war where British nurse Florence Nightingale became famous for her work with wounded soldiers.

The Ottoman Empire continued to lose land

in the Balkans (areas near Romania, Bulgaria, and Bosnia) before World War I. The once mighty Empire would become known as the "sick man of Europe."

Definition: British East India Company

This was a joint-stock company (venture where investors could buy stock in the company) that controlled much of the trade in India by the first half of the nineteenth century. As the Mughal Empire weakened, Britain continued a policy of imperialism in the subcontinent of India. Because India had a population hovering over 300 million, it was a great market for selling finished goods. Indian people were encouraged to purchase only British items. Eventually, India became known as the *"jewel in the crown,"* meaning it was the most valuable of all of the British colonial treasures.

Definition: Sepoy Mutiny, 1857

In 1857, a rebellion was caused by Indian nationalism and discontent with the British Empire. A *sepoy* was an Indian soldier of Hindu or Muslim descent who was hired to fight for the British. The spark that triggered conflict was talk of the British using grease from meat in their firearm cartridges. Since soldiers bit open these cartridges when reloading, the grease would go against the religious dietary restrictions of the sepoys. At first, protesters were thrown in jail. Later, violence ensued. The British put down the uprising, and strengthened their grip over India. Strict British rule, known as the *British Raj*, continued until 1947.

Question: Why did China break its policy of isolation?

Answer: China attempted to prevent European control. They were self-sufficient, yet traded many goods with the West. However, things changed by 1830 because of an addiction to a narcotic called opium. Millions of Chinese people became addicted to opium supplied by the British. The drug trade eventually led to war.

Definition: First Opium War, 1839-1842

Because of the drug trade mentioned above, there was extreme discontent in China. The first Opium War (there were two), saw Britain's powerful steamships and technologically advanced weapons defeat the Chinese. The war began in 1839, and the *Treaty of Nanjing* (Nanking) of 1842 gave England control of *Hong Kong*. Hong Kong would become a booming metropolis over the next century. The Chinese lost a second Opium War in 1860. In 1997, the British handed Hong Kong back to the Chinese.

Definition: Spheres of Influence

Britain wasn't the only nation who entered China. Other European countries, Japan, and the United States were also present. Each na-

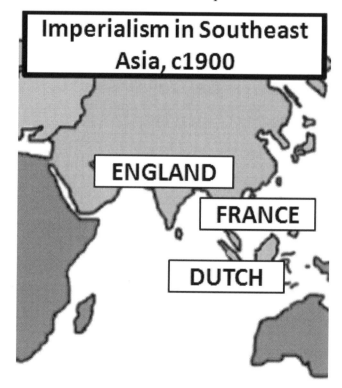

Imperialism in Southeast Asia, c1900

ENGLAND

FRANCE

DUTCH

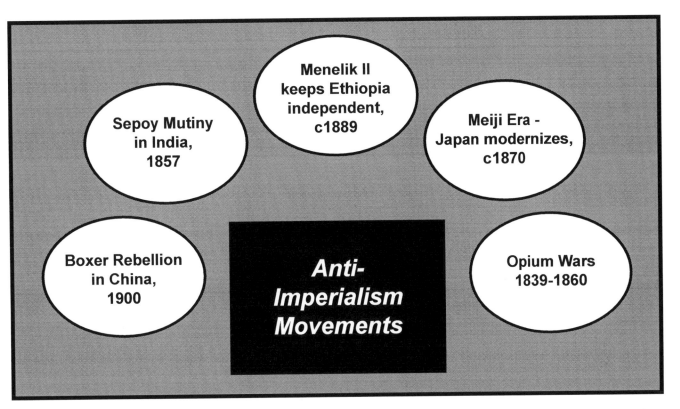

tion carved out a "sphere of influence," meaning they each began to control the trade within a piece of territory within China.

Definition: Open Door Policy, 1899

Generally, US Secretary of State John Hay's policy was created to protect American trading interests in China. The United States did not want to lose Chinese trade to other European countries, so it declared China open to all countries who wanted to trade. Of course, China could not object.

Definition: Boxer Rebellion, 1900

Boxers were Chinese people who wanted to drive out foreign imperialist nations. In addition, they resented Chinese conversions to Christianity. In 1900, they rebelled. Imperialist nations ended the uprising rather quickly. China would not rid itself of all foreign interests for another fifty years.

Decades before from 1850-64, there was a religious and political civil war called the Taiping Rebellion. It was led by Chinese Christians who wanted to redistribute wealth across the country. The Qing Dynasty put down the rebellion with the help of European powers.

Question: How did Japan's experiences with imperialism differ from those of China?

Answer: Whereas China did not adapt to westernization, Japan did. In 1853, American Commodore Matthew Perry landed in Tokyo. Japan had no choice but to open its once isolated doors to trade. However, unlike China, Japan industrialized and grew stronger. When shogun rule ended in 1867, the emperor was returned to power in the Meiji Restoration. Japanese Emperor Mutsuhito looked to enlighten Japan with modernization.

In the *Meiji Era* from 1868-1912, the Japanese embraced Western technology and modernized their factories. They began to model their government and economy after the West.

Unlike the Chinese who were imperialized, the Japanese *became* imperialists. Because Japan did not have extensive reserves of resources, they looked elsewhere for raw materials. Remember: M for Meiji. M for Modernization.

Question: Where did the Japanese imperialize?

Answer: The Japanese fought several wars. You should know:

1. Sino-Japanese War, 1894-95 - Japan swiftly defeated the Chinese and took some land.

2. Russo-Japanese War, 1904-05 - Japan's victory over the much larger Russia shocked the world. The war paved the way for Japan's eventual domination of Northern China (Manchuria) and Korea. In both places, the Japanese ruled harshly and enforced their culture upon the imperialized.

• WORLD WAR I
Question: What were the causes for The Great War (World War I)?

Answer: Mnemonic device: **MANIA**

M - **M**ilitarism - European nations began amassing large armies that were prepared for war.

A - **A**lliances - These militarized nations created alliances. Germany, Austria-Hungary, and Italy joined the Triple Alliance in 1882. Russia, France, and Britain entered the Triple Entente in 1907.

N - **N**ationalism - Different nations believed that they should dominate the European continent.

I - **I**mperialism - Nations wanted to gain territory and make their Empires more powerful.

A - **A**ssassination - The spark that started the war was the assassination of *Archduke Franz Ferdinand* who was shot by Serbian nationalist Gavrilo Princip on June 28, 1914. Serbia was one of the nations breaking away from the "powder keg" or "sick man" of Europe...the Ottoman Empire.

After the assassination, Austria-Hungary declared war on Serbia, and a *chain reaction* of war declarations spread throughout Europe.

Question: What military events of World War I (1914-1918) are important to know?

Answer:

1. The war was fought on both the Western and Eastern Fronts. The Western Front was on the French and German border. The Eastern Front was on the German/Austro-Hungarian and Russian border.

2. The Triple Entente became known as the Allies. The Triple Alliance lost Italy, and became the Central Powers (Germany and Austria-Hungary).

3. The early German strategy was called the Schlieffen Plan. Its goal was to swiftly defeat France, and then move eastward to defeat Russia. This never happened.

4. Russia dropped out of the war because of the Russian Revolution (explained in next chapter).

5. The war moved outside of the two European fronts, as Gallipoli in modern-day Turkey (Ottoman Empire) saw fierce fighting.

6. Months after American reinforcements arrived, Kaiser Wilhelm II signed an *armistice* to end the fighting on November 11, 1918 (the eleventh hour of the eleventh day in the eleventh month).

Question: What caused the United States to enter World War I in 1917?

Answer: Before the war, the United States remained neutral. However, certain international events changed this. It's good to know... *The Boat and The Note.*

1. The Boat - The *Lusitania*. It was a passenger ship sailing off the coast of Ireland. It was

sunk by a German submarine (U-boat) on May 7, 1915. The US warned Germany to refrain from continued submarine warfare. However, the Germans would not stop.

2. The Note - *The Zimmermann Telegram*. In 1917, the British intercepted a telegram from Arthur Zimmermann of Germany. He was writing to Mexico seeking an alliance. The Germans proposed that, if victorious at the end of the war, land from the United States would be given to Mexico.

The Germans continued their policy of unrestricted submarine warfare. President Woodrow Wilson asked Congress to declare war in April of 1917. He was hoping to make the world "safe for democracy."

Question: What were the technological innovations of World War I?

Answer: This modern war saw:

1. Trench Warfare - Though used in earlier wars, trenches were most prevalent in World War I. Trenches involved the digging of large holes/tunnels in the ground. They were used to take cover from enemy fire. Ultimately in World War I, soldiers could not move very far in a day, as new trenches would have to be dug. The trenches were filthy, and full of vermin and disease.

2. *U-boats* (Unterseeboots), or submarines - The Germans enhanced the invention of the submarine. They used these U-boats to sink ships and control the high seas early in the war.

3. Airplane - The Wright brothers of the United States successfully flew the first flight in 1903. A decade later, the plane was able to drop bombs, spy, fight, and transport materials.

4. Poison/Mustard Gas and Gasmasks - A German innovation that was soon used by the Allies, chemical weapons were common in the Great War. Gasmasks were used by both sides to prevent respiratory failure.

5. Tanks - A British invention. Early tanks were not very reliable. However the Germans would improve on the technology during World War II.

6. Machine guns and flamethrowers were also used in this war.

Definition: Fourteen Points

United States President Woodrow Wilson presented his plan for peace. In a 1918 speech, Wilson addressed issues of fair trade, freedom of the seas, treatment of the imperialized, and constructing new borders. Most important was his fourteenth point, which was to create an international peace-keeping organization. This would become the *League of Nations*. Unlike today's United Nations, the League could not raise an army to enforce peace.

Definition: Treaty of Versailles, June 28, 1919

The *Big Four* who helped influence the peace treaty were Woodrow Wilson of the US, David Lloyd George of Britain, Georges Clemenceau of France, and Vittorio Orlando of Italy. The Treaty of Versailles was signed on the fifth anniversary of the Ferdinand assassination. In the treaty:

1. Germany lost Alsace-Lorraine to the French. They also surrendered other international colonies.

2. Germany had to shrink the size of its army and could not manufacture weapons. In addition, they had to stop constructing U-boats.

3. Germany was found guilty of causing the war and had to pay $33 billion in war reparations.

This harsh treatment of Germany in the aftermath of the war has led many historians to believe that the Treaty of Versailles was a cause for World War II.

Note: The United States never ratified the

Treaty of Versailles because the US Senate feared that joining the League of Nations would encroach on their neutrality.

Question: What were some territorial changes in Europe after World War I?

Answer:

1. Austria-Hungary became Austria, Hungary, and Czechoslovakia. Some land would eventually become Yugoslavia.

2. After dropping out of the war, Russia lost what would become Estonia, Ukraine, Finland, Latvia, and Lithuania.

3. Poland, which was not a nation when the war began, became independent.

4. What had been the Ottoman Empire became Turkey. Turkey's independence movement was led by ***Mustafa Kemal Atatürk***. He became the first president of the Republic of Turkey in 1923, and transformed the country into a secular state (not controlled by Islam). He helped bring women equality under the law, and encouraged them to give up their veils and dress in Western clothes. Women also received full political rights, including suffrage.

Definition Armenian Massacres

Before World War I, the Christian Armenian population demanded rights within the Ottoman Empire. They were met with military resistance. Many were killed. During and after World War I, Armenians suffered deportation, starvation, forced marches, torture, and execution. An estimated one million people were killed in the atrocities. The killing ended in 1923. Though considered by some to be genocide, the Turkish government denied such claims.

Review Questions

1. Which of the following was true of imperialism in China and Japan?
A) Rebellions in Japan were successful and prevented European contact
B) China quickly industrialized which led to the exit of imperial powers
C) Japan's Meiji Restoration gradually turned them into an imperialistic threat
D) The British could not capitalize on the opium and tea trade in China

2. Which of these African nations remained independent from European rule by 1900?
A) Sudan
B) South Africa
C) Congo
D) Ethiopia

3. What was one outcome of the Boer War?
A) The end of British control in the western regions of Africa
B) British domination in the Union of South Africa
C) British control of the Congo River as an outlet to the Atlantic Ocean
D) A decreased need for Britain to utilize Asian tea markets

4. Which of the following saw a gradual loss of power from 1850 to World War I?
A) Gupta Empire
B) Ottoman Empire
C) Second Reich
D) Austro-Hungarian Empire

5. The "jewel in the crown" of the British Empire was
A) Egypt
B) Japan
C) China
D) India

6. The outcome of the Opium Wars was
A) decreased British imperialism in the eastern regions of China
B) an elimination of American spheres of influence in China
C) a transferring of Hong Kong to British hands
D) the end of Chinese conversions to Christianity

7. Which of the following was the spark that led to a chain reaction of war in 1914?
A) The sinking of the *Lusitania*
B) Assassination of Archduke Franz Ferdinand
C) German militarization in a time of peace
D) Unrestricted and ruthless submarine attacks in the Atlantic

8. The Schlieffen Plan was
A) a German war goal to quickly defeat France, and then shift attention to Russia
B) an Allied strategy to gain land in the Balkans
C) a proposed alliance between Germany and Mexico
D) the transformation of World War I from a battle on land, to one in the air

9. The Treaty of Versailles looked to do all of the following EXCEPT:

A) Limit the manufacturing of weapons in Germany

B) Remove Alsace-Lorraine from German hands

C) Allow for an international army to enforce the Treaty

D) Penalize Germany a large sum of money for their war guilt

10. After World War I, which of the following countries was established from the former Austro-Hungarian Empire?

A) Lithuania

B) Estonia

C) Latvia

D) Czechoslovakia

Answers and Explanations

. **C**. During the Meiji Era, Japan gradually industrialized. By 1900, they were an international force and started to imperialize neighboring countries.

. **D**. After the Berlin Conference divided up Africa among European powers, Menelik II helped Ethiopia remain independent from imperial rule. Liberia also stayed independent.

. **B**. The Boers were Dutch settlers in Southern Africa. The British defeated the Boers in a series of conflicts, and took control of what would become the Union of South Africa.

. **B**. The Ottoman Empire was known as the "sick man of Europe," as it was slowly deteriorating by the twentieth century.

. **D**. With a market containing millions of people, India was the most valuable of all of the British colonial treasures.

6. **C**. The Chinese handed over Hong Kong in the Treaty of Nanjing. They would not get it back until 1997.

7. **B**. The assassination of Archduke Franz Ferdinand was the spark that led to a chain reaction that erupted into World War I.

8. **A**. Strong German nationalism led to the belief that the Central Powers could quickly defeat France, and then focus their attention on Russia in the East. However, they were never able to defeat the Allies on the Western Front.

9. **C**. The League of Nations had no army. The United Nations would have one after World War II.

10. **D**. Czechoslovakia came out of the Austro-Hungarian Empire. The other choices were from Russia.

The Russian Revolution and Joseph Stalin

By the mid-twentieth century, the Soviet Union's importance in global affairs was immense. However in 1900, Russia was industrially backwards and ruled by czars incapable of providing for the welfare of the common people. The first two decades of the twentieth century led to the deaths of millions, as revolution, World War I, civil war, famine, and harsh living conditions took a toll on the Russian people. When the dust settled, a new nation emerged called the Soviet Union. Under the leadership of Vladimir Lenin, and later Joseph Stalin, the Soviet Union became the largest communist state in the world. Its emergence coincided with the sacrifice of individual rights and liberties.

HERE IS WHAT YOU NEED TO KNOW:
Definition: Pogroms

Under Czar Alexander III, there was a hope to unify Russian culture. This meant persecution of the many Jews who lived in the country. Pogroms were organized massacres that targeted them. Jews were also removed to an area of Russia known as the pale of settlement. *Anti-Semitism* caused many to emigrate from Russia in the early twentieth century.

Definition: Czar Nicholas II

Nicholas Romanov would be the last czar of Russia. During his reign there was massive industrialization. Specifically, the Trans-Siberian Railway became the longest rail project in the world. However, Nicholas fell out of favor with the people because of the following:

1. Russo-Japanese War, 1904-05. Besides giving up some land, the Russian people were embarrassed after losing a war to the small island of Japan.

2. *Bloody Sunday*, January 22, 1905 - When thousands of workers protested for labor rights in St. Petersburg, the Czar's Imperial Guard fired on the crowd. The backlash to this event led to the creation of a Russian parliament known as the Duma. Though it was supposed to help legislate for more rights, it didn't have much power.

3. World War I misfortune - Russia suffered the most casualties in the war, with nearly 2 million soldiers killed. Russia proved ill-equipped for battle, as they lacked military supplies and sufficient food for its troops. Nicholas went to the front lines to try to boost morale.

Definition: Grigori Rasputin

Rasputin was a "holy man" who claimed to have mystical powers. The Czar's son suffered from hemophilia, a blood disease. When Rasputin appeared to ease the boy's symptoms, Czarina Alexandra rewarded him with political power. While Nicholas was away fighting the war, Rasputin had his hand in the government and corruption became a large problem. Rasputin was ultimately murdered by aristocrats and thrown into the Neva River in 1916.

Definition: March Revolution, 1917

The workers rose up to protest both the working conditions and the misfortunes of the Great War. The Czar was stripped of power and a temporary *Provisional Government* was put in his place under the direction of Alexander Kerensky. This government proved weak. When they continued to press on fighting the war, it angered socialist groups of workers called *soviets*.

Definition: Vladimir Lenin and the Bolsheviks

Lenin was the leader of the *Bolsheviks*.

evolutionaries who turned to the writings of Karl Marx. They believed that socialism was the answer to the poor living conditions and discontent of the Russian people. Lenin had previously fled Russia, but returned when the Czar abdicated the throne. He and the popular Bolsheviks had an opportunity to seize power.

Definition: November (Bolshevik) Revolution, 1917

Lenin hoped to bring the Russian people, *"Peace, Land, and Bread."* He and the Bolsheviks overthrew the Provisional Government to gain control of Russia. To make sure the Czar's supporters didn't restore him to the throne, the entire royal family was executed in 1918. The capital of Russia was soon moved from St. Petersburg to Moscow.

Question: How did Lenin deliver on his promise of Peace, Land, and Bread?

Answer:

Peace - The 1918 *Treaty of Brest-Litovsk* allowed Russia to drop out of World War I. They gave up western land to achieve this.

Land and Bread - Lenin began to divide up all of the farms and factories amongst the people. This upset the many *kulaks*, or wealthier Russians.

Definition: Russian Civil War, 1918-1921

Leon Trotsky led the Bolshevik Red Army against the anti-Bolshevik White Army. Between the fighting, famine, and disease, more Russians were killed in this war than in World War I. Estimates range from 10-15 million. The Red Army won the war and the Bolsheviks continued to rule Russia.

Definition: New Economic Policy, 1921

After the war, Lenin set up *NEP*. NEP permitted some capitalism, as shopkeepers were allowed to keep small profits. However, the government remained in control of most production in the factory system.

Definition: Communism in the USSR

The Bolshevik Party changed its name to the Communist Party. Communism was a system supported by the writer Karl Marx. This is a government that provides a classless society where the workers share the means of production. Communism became a dictatorship under Lenin. With Joseph Stalin, this dictatorship grew stronger.

In 1922, Russia and surrounding lands such as Ukraine and Belarus became the *Union of Soviet Socialist Republics* (USSR). It can also be called the *Soviet Union*. This enormous area extended into northern Asia. A movement called *Russification* attempted to expand the Russian culture and language to areas far away from Moscow.

Definition: Joseph Stalin and Totalitarianism

Joseph Stalin worked his way up the Communist Party and took control of it by 1928. Stalin was a harsh dictator who ruled through *totalitarianism*. Totalitarianism occurs when a government not only takes over the economic and political lives of the people, but their social rights as well. Stalin controlled production, the media, the economy, and everything else under the Soviet sun. Churches were destroyed, and *atheism* (rejection of a belief in God) was advised. Those who went against Stalin were either killed or sent to a labor camp known as a *gulag*.

Under Stalin's regime, women entered the workplace. Communist law gave women equal rights. Despite working long days in the socialist economy, women were also instrumental in raising children and running the home.

Definition: Command Economy/First Five-Year Plan, 1928

Stalin commanded the economy, meaning he made all regulations for agriculture and industry. Regarding industry, Stalin made a series of *Five-Year Plans* which aimed to modernize the Soviet Union, as it lagged behind other European countries. The plan looked to produce raw materials such as coal and iron, and extend railway lines, electricity, and communication networks. Production from factories increased, but they never met the impossible quotas that Stalin set out to achieve. In addition, unlike in capitalist nations, there was a lack of consumer goods being produced in the Soviet Union.

In the command economy, Stalin seized all of the privately owned farms and made them *collective farms*. This obviously upset the landowners, known as kulaks. Many were executed during the collectivization process.

Definition: The Great Purge of the 1930s

Stalin was very paranoid of his enemies… and his former friends. Because of this, he targeted any official whom he *thought* could be a traitor. To purge means to remove or kill. His secret police rounded up suspected enemies of the state, and they were either murdered or shipped to a gulag. The Great Purge targeted government officials in the Communist Party and peasants who were seen as enemies of the state. After unfair trials, most were executed. The killings peaked from 1937-38.

Religious structures were destroyed in favor of statues celebrating Marx, Engels, Lenin, and Stalin

It is believed that Joseph Stalin killed more people than Adolf Hitler. Estimates are as high as 20 million. Through fear and immense *propaganda* (biased media coverage, posters, school curriculum, speeches, and parades), Stalin *indoctrinated* the people of Russia. This meant that his views were accepted as truth. All opposition was silenced.

Review Questions

1. Under Czar Alexander's rule, Jews in Russia were

A) given equal citizenship rights

B) permitted religious tolerance

C) targeted with organized violence

D) forced to work as serfs on the Trans-Siberian Railway

2. Bloody Sunday was a violent response against Russians who wanted

A) more rights for the working class

B) religious toleration

C) an end to Russification

D) collectivization of private farms

3. Vladimir Lenin's rise to power was related to all of the following EXCEPT:

A) Discontent with czarist rule

B) Dissatisfaction with labor conditions and a low standard of living

C) World War I's devastating effects on the Russian people

D) Support from the Eastern Orthodox Church

4. The Bolshevik Revolutionaries supported the

A) limiting of workers' rights

B) Provisional Government of Alexander Kerensky

C) Russian tradition of Czarist rule

D) writings of Karl Marx

5. Vladimir Lenin's New Economic Policy

A) permitted a few private businesses to profit

B) advocated for full-scale capitalism

C) denied peasants the ownership of livestock

D) led to full scale unionization of workers

6. In a command economy

A) unionization of workers is encouraged by the government

B) the government can regulate prices, but not materials produced

C) agricultural ventures are given preference over industry

D) the leader of the nation-state determines what is produced

7. Which of the following was true of Joseph Stalin's Five-Year Plan of 1928?

A) It was the only one of its kind during Stalin's reign as leader

B) Stalin set quotas so high, that they could not be met

C) The Soviet Union became the world leader in industrialization by 1933

D) Major advances in consumer goods came out of the Soviet Union for the first time

8. Kulaks were those who

A) helped Stalin rise to the top of the Communist Party

B) accumulated land and resisted the collectivization process

C) policed the labor camps, or gulags

D) advised Stalin on industrial measures

9. Joseph Stalin supported all of the following EXCEPT:

A) Atheism
B) Propaganda in schools
C) Totalitarianism
D) Free thought in literature

10. Women in the Soviet Union

A) could not give birth to more than one child
B) were forbidden to work industrial jobs
C) gained education and entered the work force
D) were not permitted to work in the medical profession

Answers and Explanations

C. Jews suffered from the organized violence of the pogroms. They were also forced to live in a special area known as the pale of settlement.

A. Bloody Sunday was a violent reaction to a workers' protest in St. Petersburg. The Czar's Imperial Guard opened fire on the protesters.

D. Much like Stalin, Lenin did not support organized religion in the socialist state.

D. The writings of Karl Marx, notably the *Communist Manifesto*, helped inspire the Bolshevik Revolution.

A. Lenin's NEP allowed for a small amount of capitalism to take place.

D. In a command economy, the leader of the nation-state dictates the economy. In the case of the Soviet Union in 1928, that dictator was Joseph Stalin.

7. **B.** Stalin set quotas quite high. Many of the reported production numbers were embellished during the Five-Year Plans out of fear of upsetting Stalin. Stalin would put through a series of Five-Year plans as leader of the Soviet Union.

8. **B.** Kulaks were wealthy Russians who had nothing to gain from the collectivization effort. Kulaks lost their land, as it was redistributed to the peasants. Many were executed or sent to gulags.

9. **D.** Stalin was notorious for censoring any thought that criticized or undermined his totalitarian rule. He was in complete control of the media.

10. **C.** Similar to what would happen in China under Mao Zedong, women actually gained rights during communist rule. However, they were expected to not only work, but raise families as well.

Fascism, World War II, and the Holocaust

World War I was supposed to be the worst war in history. However, about twenty years after it ended, a second and more deadly war encompassed the globe. Reacting to discontent, nationalism, and economic depression, people rallied behind fascist dictators in Italy and Germany. When both nations aligned with the equally ambitious Japanese Emperor, the Axis Powers were formed. Their thirst for land and power led to invasions of their neighbors. World War II lasted in Europe from 1939-1945. As Germany was attempting to expand, they were committing horrific atrocities to the Jewish population of Europe. The tragedy of the Holocaust was made known to the world after the Allies defeated the Axis in World War II.

HERE IS WHAT YOU NEED TO KNOW:

• FASCISM
Definition: Fascism

Fascism became popular in certain European countries between the World Wars. It is a political ideology where a dictator promotes nationalism under the threat of extensive military force. A fascist dictator controls nearly all aspects of life within a nation. Fascism grew out of discontent and desperation in the years following World War I.

Question: What happened to the world economy after World War I?

Answer: A global depression developed in the 1920s, and the new governments formed after World War I struggled to cope with it. Specifically, in Germany, the new democratic *Weimar Republic* attempted to handle their economic problems by printing more money. This devalued the currency, as immense infla-

tion occurred. This further made the economy spiral out of control. In Italy, there was also immense unemployment and high inflation.

Even in the United States there was a Great Depression by 1929, as farmers overproduced crops, banks faile[d] and the stock market crashed. Franklin Delan[o] Roosevelt was elected President and attempte[d] vast reform measures with his *New Deal*. H[is] hope was to repair the banking system and cre[e]ate jobs through government-sponsored build[d]ing projects.

Question: Why was Benito Mussolini able [to] rise to power in Italy?

Answer: Mussolini was a fascist dictator [in] Italy from 1922 through most of World War I[I.] He was able to rise because:

1. There was extreme discontent that cam[e] with the economic depression following Wor[ld] War I.

2. There was a fear of a workers' communi[st] revolt, as Italy favored capitalism.

3. There was immense nationalism, as even[n]tually Mussolini would play off of the histo[ry] of the great Roman Empire. After seizing pow[w]er, he would sometimes give speeches at th[e] Roman Colosseum.

Mussolini and his army of Blacksh[irts] *marched on Rome* in 1922. King Emmanu[el] III gave Mussolini control of the governme[nt] under the threat of violence. Mussolini took [on] a new title, *Il Duce* (The Leader).

Question: How did Mussolini control th[e] government?

Answer: Like Stalin, Mussolini had a secr[et] police which eliminated all opponents. He pr[o]hibited strikes, controlled the economy, an[d] made Roman Catholicism the favored religi[on] f Italy as per the *Lateran Pacts* (agreements with the Church). All opposition to the Fascist Party was controlled.

Question: Why was Adolf Hitler able to rise to power in Germany?

Answer: Adolf Hitler secured power under a fascist regime from 1933 through World War II. He was able to rise because:

1. There was economic discontent that came out of the depression.

2. The punishments of the Treaty of Versailles left many Germans angered. This sparked nationalism.

3. Regarding nationalism, people rallied behind the words of Hitler. He was arrested in 1923 for attempting a revolt in Munich, Germany. From prison he wrote *Mein Kampf* (My Struggle). In the book, he explained how he thought Germany should be governed. Furthermore, he spoke of the German *master race* of *Aryans*, whom he believed were superior to Jews and other minorities in Germany. His nationalistic tone, and his call for increasing the *living space (lebensraum)* of Germany, gave the book immense appeal among Germans.

4. The Weimar Republic was a weak and inefficient democracy. As stated earlier, the economy under the Weimar Republic was strangled with inflation after the government printed up too much money.

5. There was a fear of communism in Germany. Before a 1933 election, Hitler's *Nazi Party* (National Socialist Party) set fire to the *Reichstag* (parliament) and blamed the torching on the communists. This propaganda lie helped the Nazis secure more seats in government.

Question: How did Hitler control the government?

Answer: In 1933, Hitler became Chancellor of Germany and took on the title of *Der Führer* (The Leader). Enemies were targeted through both Heinrich Himmler's military, the *SS* (Schutzstaffel), and the *Gestapo* (secret state police). Similar to other dictators, Hitler commanded the economy and increased the manufacture of industry and weapons. Also, like other leaders, Hitler encouraged a great deal of propaganda, which increased support for the Nazi Party. With the help of Propaganda Minister *Joseph Goebbels*, a "big lie" was created through radio, posters, school control, speeches, and parades. Everywhere, flags with the Nazi *swastika* symbol could be seen. Literature that went against Nazi ideals was banned or burned.

Hitler's *Third Reich* (name of his government) produced much nationalism. It was believed that the Aryans were the master race, and there should be racial purity and no intermingling of races. Jews were persecuted (explained later). The Nazis also relied on the century-old philosophy of German *Friedrich Nietzsche*. They selectively quoted him to criticize democracy. Nietzsche was an *existentialist*, meaning he stressed that an individual's existence is based on self-determination and free-choice.

Definition: Francisco Franco, Spain

Spain became engaged in a civil war in 1936 when Francisco Franco's fascist Nationalist Army attempted to seize power. Hitler and Mussolini both supported Franco, and the Spanish government was overthrown in 1939. Franco was in office until 1975. Spain gradually moved to democracy after his death.

Question: What territories did Germany secure under Hitler?

Answer: Because the League of Nations had no army to stop him, Hitler disobeyed the Treaty of Versailles and increased the size of his army. Germany remilitarized the Rhineland on its western border (which was in violation of the Treaty). In addition, Hitler annexed (added to Germany) Austria through a process called *Anschluss*.

Hitler also wanted the *Sudetenland*, an area of Czechoslovakia where the people spoke German. He was given this territory at the 1938 *Munich Conference*. There, British Prime Minister Neville Chamberlain said that the transfer of land would give the world "peace in our time." He was wrong, as it only made Hitler hungry for more. The Munich Conference is an example of *appeasement*, or meeting the aggressor's demands to keep peace.

Definition: Nazi-Soviet Nonaggression Pact, 1939

Remember: Russia was Napoleon's ally. Napoleon invaded Russia. Napoleon lost. The same would be true of Hitler. In 1939, the Soviets and Germans agreed not to attack each other. Because both powers were natural enemies, many were doubtful this agreement would last. It didn't.

Definition: Axis Powers

As Hitler and the Nazis were gaining territory, so too were Japan and Italy. Japan had been in Manchuria, (northern) China since 1931. Under *Emperor Hirohito*, Japan continued to gain land and commit atrocities on the Chinese people. In particular, the Nanjing Massacre of 1937 (also known as the Rape of Nanjing) involved the slaughtering of about 300,000 Chinese prisoners of war and civilians, including the rape and execution of thousands of women.

Italy fought to gain control of Haile Selassie's Ethiopia. Although Ethiopia was able to remain free from Italian control during the Age of Imperialism in the late nineteenth century, they

fell to Mussolini in 1936. That same year, alliance known as the *Axis Powers* was form between Japan, Italy, and Germany.

• WORLD WAR II
Question: What important diplomacy curred before and during the war?

Answer: In between the World Wars: T *Washington Naval Conference* of 1921 s the major powers agree to limit naval arn The *Kellogg-Briand Pact* of 1928 renounc war as a form of national policy.

The United States and President Frank Roosevelt remained *neutral* before the w America's Neutrality Acts of 1935, 1937, a 1939 kept them neutral, mostly in terms arms shipments to foreign countries. "Ca and Carry" was a 1939 policy proclaimi that America would aid Great Britain. Th was only if the British came to the US on th own ships, paid in cash, and then left with t weapons. Finally, in the Destroyers for Bas Deal of 1940, Roosevelt *traded* older lar ships (destroyers) in exchange for British ba es in the Caribbean.

Of greater importance was the *Lend-Lea Act* of 1941. This act allowed the United Stat to sell unlimited weapons to the Allies. T buying was done on credit. Over $50 billion supplies were sent overseas (to Britain, Sovi Union, France, and China).

Definition: Invasion of Poland and Blit krieg

World War II in Europe began on Septemb 1, 1939 when the Nazis invaded Poland. Th did this in a surprise *blitzkrieg*, or "lightnir war," that used immense air and land force Poland quickly fell. Great Britain and Fran declared war on Germany. Note: Many histor ans consider the beginning of the war to be 1931 when Japan invaded Manchuria, China

Question: What were the important events World War II in Europe from 1940-1942?

Answer:

1. France fell to Germany quickly in 1940. *Charles de Gaulle*, a leader of the Free French Forces, evacuated to Britain. Other Allies escaped as well after the Battle of Dunkirk.

2. Germany bombed Britain in 1940, but stopped in 1941 after strong resistance from the RAF (Royal Air Force). Much of London's population, including Prime Minister *Winston Churchill*, fled underground to stay safe during the Battle of Britain.

3. In 1941, Hitler invaded the Soviet Union in *Operation Barbarossa*, thus breaking the nonaggression pact. The Germans never took Moscow. After the *Battle of Stalingrad* in 1942, the Soviets pushed back the German offensive. The harsh Russian winter played a great part in Germany's withdrawal. Like Napoleon over a century earlier, the German army had a hard time mobilizing.

Definition: Pearl Harbor

On December 7, 1941 the Japanese attacked the United States by air at Pearl Harbor in Hawaii. The sneak-attack resulted in 2,300 American soldiers killed, many of whom were aboard the USS *Arizona*.

After Franklin Roosevelt's "Day of Infamy" speech, Congress declared war on Japan. Shortly after, Germany declared war on the US. During the course of the war, the United States, Britain, France, and the Soviet Union were the major Allies who fought the Axis Powers.

Question: What military events in Europe should I know about from 1942-1945?

Answer:

1. The United States began fighting in northern Africa and then went further north to liberate Italy. Mussolini was executed by his own people after falling from power.

2. *D-Day*, June 6, 1944, was the largest battle and the turning point of the war. It led to the liberation of France. American General Dwight Eisenhower was the Allied Commander.

3. The Battle of the Bulge during the winter of 1944-45 was the deadliest battle in Europe for the Americans. However, Germany could not permanently break Allied lines.

4. Adolf Hitler committed suicide in an underground bunker on April 30, 1945. V-E (Victory in Europe) Day would be on May 8th after Germany surrendered.

Definition: Yalta Conference, 1945

The Yalta Conference gave the Soviet Union control over much of Eastern Europe. Though the Soviets promised free elections, these promises were empty, as the nations were turned into satellites. It can be said that Yalta was the start of the Cold War.

In the conference, it was also agreed that the Soviets would enter the war in Japan, and Germany would be divided into zones of occupation. This Conference, held in the Soviet Union, occurred in the final days of President Roosevelt's life. When he died soon after, Vice President Harry Truman took over.

Other conferences to know about:

1. Tehran, 1943 - Here, the Allies planned the end of the war strategy to defeat the Nazis.

2. Potsdam, 1945 - The Allies discussed the fate of Germany after they surrendered.

Question: What do I need to know about the War in the Pacific (Japan)?

Answer:

1. American General Douglas MacArthur was the commander.

2. The United States followed a strategy of *island hopping* before reaching mainland Japan. Some of the islands attacked were Mid-

way, Iwo Jima, and Okinawa.

3. President Truman decided a mainland invasion of Japan would be too costly in terms of casualties, so he put in the order for the *Enola Gay* to drop *Little Boy* (the Atomic Bomb). On August 6, 1945 Hiroshima was bombed resulting in the deaths of about 140,000 people. Nagasaki was bombed three days later leading to an estimated 70,000 deaths.

4. Japan surrendered on August 15, 1945. V-J (Victory in Japan) Day would be on September 2nd.

Question: What were the foreign policy results of World War II?

Answer: An estimated 60 million people were killed in World War II, with over 1/3 of all casualties occurring among people in the Soviet Union. In the aftermath of the worst war in world history:

1. The US and Soviet Union became superpowers, and the Cold War began.

2. Germany was divided into occupational zones controlled by the Soviet Union in the East, and Allies (Britain, France, and the United States) in the West.

3. The *United Nations* was formed as an international peacekeeping organization. The US, Soviet Union, France, Britain, and China would be the Five Permanent Nations with veto power. The UN grew out of the *Atlantic Charter* of 1941, where Winston Churchill and Franklin Roosevelt agreed to stabilize the world with peace once the war ended. Unlike the League of Nations, the UN can assemble peacekeeping troops. Also, unlike the League, the US joined the UN.

4. The US demilitarized Japan and forced them to adopt a new constitution modeled after the American two-house legislature. Japan was forbidden to wage offensive wars. The US occupied Japan until 1951. In the ensuing decades, Japan industrialized and became worldwide economic power. They also becam a firm ally of the United States.

• THE HOLOCAUST
Definition: Nuremberg Laws, 1935

These were German laws in the 1930s th labeled Jews as inferiors who could not ho government jobs, nor marry non-Jewish Ge mans. Therefore, Jews were second-class cit zens. When World War II began in Europe 1939, they were forced to wear yellow badg in the shape of the Star of David.

To avoid persecution, many Jews fled to th United States and elsewhere abroad. Howeve nations began to close their doors to immigr tion. One who escaped Germany was phys cist Albert Einstein. Creator of the *Theory Relativity* that questioned the traditional lav of time and space, Einstein also recommend that the United States develop an atomic bom The Manhattan Project would become the co name for this operation.

Jews were forced to wear yellow Stars of David during War. Jüde is German for Jew.

The above sign at the concentration camp at Terezin translates to "work sets you free." This was an unfulfilled promise.

Definition: Kristallnacht, 1938

Kristallnacht translates to "night of broken glass." On November 9, 1938 Nazi soldiers attacked Jews, their homes, and their synagogues. Thousands of Jewish establishments were burned and vandalized all over Germany and Austria. The violence was triggered when a Jewish man named Herschel Grynszpan assassinated a German government worker.

Definition: Ghettos

Like the pogroms of Russia c1900, German Jews were forced to live in reserved areas (mostly in Poland). The Nazis sealed the borders of these ghettos leading to starvation and disease. Still, Jews were able to smuggle in necessities such as food, and religious materials.

Definition: Warsaw Uprising

Warsaw is the capital of Poland. The largest revolt of Jews during the Holocaust occurred in the Warsaw Ghetto in 1943. With limited weapons, Jews held off the Nazis for about one month before the Germans put down the uprising. The resistance became a symbol of Jewish solidarity and defiance.

Definition: The Final Solution

As the war progressed, the elimination of Jews became a priority for the Nazis. The Final Solution was *genocide*, or the methodical killing of an entire group of people. Those seen as undesirable or inferior to the master race of Aryans were targeted. Jews, Gypsies, homosexuals, the mentally ill, and others were murdered.

The killing was done in *concentration camps* and *extermination camps*. Many died in concentration camps through slave labor. Later in the war, extermination camps, such as Auschwitz in Poland, were used for the purpose of killing. A chemical named Zyklon B was used to murder Jews in showers. The bodies were then sent to crematoriums. An estimated 6 million Jews were killed in the Holocaust, and 11 million people overall. Most of the victims were from Poland and the Soviet Union.

The camps were liberated by the Allies in 1945. The reason why so many of the horrors of the Holocaust are known today is because of *primary sources,* or firsthand accounts. Survivors such as *Elie Wiesel*, who wrote *Night*, have made sure that the atrocities are still remembered in the twenty-first century.

Definition: Anne Frank

Anne Frank lived in Amsterdam in the Netherlands. Like many Jews, she and her family hid from Nazi officers. Anne kept a diary where she detailed the experiences of hiding out in an annex (attic). The diary has become one of the most famous primary sources available on the Holocaust. Anne and her family were captured at the end of the war. Anne did not survive the Holocaust.

Definition: Nuremberg Trials

After the war ended in 1945, 22 Nazis were charged with war crimes. 12 were sentenced to death. Hundreds of Nazi officers associated with concentration or extermination camps were never tried for crimes against humanity.

Which decision by the Weimar Republic used the greatest harm to the German economy?
A) increasing taxes
B) purchasing foreign bonds
C) printing more money
D) raising tariffs

A similarity between Adolf Hitler and Benito ussolini was
A) a strong belief in socialism
B) support for unionization of workers
C) use of propaganda techniques
D) persecution of Roman Catholics

In *Mein Kampf*, Adolf Hitler supported
A) securing the Sudetenland through appeasement
B) enforcing the provisions of the Treaty of Versailles
C) the extermination of Russians and Poles
D) a master race of Aryans superior to Jews

Which nation is paired with the territory they ok over in the 1930s?
A) Germany - Ethiopia
B) Japan - Manchuria
C) Italy - Rhineland
D) Austria - Turkey

5. The United States ended their policies of neutrality in the 1940s when
A) The Japanese attacked Pearl Harbor
B) Germany continued a policy of unrestricted submarine warfare
C) Italy declared war on the United States
D) United States boats were sunk in the Atlantic

6. Put the following events of World War II in chronological order
1. German blitzkrieg of Poland
2. Dropping of the Atomic Bomb on Hiroshima
3. Japan attacks Pearl Harbor
4. France falls to Hitler

A) 1-2-4-3
B) 4-1-3-2
C) 4-1-2-3
D) 1-4-3-2

7. The turning point of World War II in Western Europe occurred in the
A) Invasion of Normandy
B) Battle of the Bulge
C) Battle of Stalingrad
D) Battle of London

8. The Yalta Conference presented which potential conflict for Europe?
A) A struggle for land between Britain and the United States
B) The spread of communism throughout Eastern Europe
C) The unification of Germany
D) A nuclear arms race between Western nations

9. The Nuremberg Laws of 1935 persecuted Jews by

A) denying basic freedoms

B) removing them to ghettos during World War II

C) ordering their removal to extermination camps in Poland

D) deporting them to the United States

10. Elie Wiesel's records of World War II have been important because they

A) give a clear picture of the Battle of Stalingrad

B) prove that Hitler died in an underground bunker

C) detail the atrocities of the Holocaust

D) display the importance of the airplane during World War II

C. To combat economic problems after
rld War I, the Weimar Republic of Germany
nted up more money. When they did this,
ssive inflation occurred.

C. Both fascist leaders used elaborate pa-
les, salutes, and speeches to promote nation-
sm among their people. Joseph Goebbels in
rmany created a *big lie* using propaganda.

D. Hitler wrote *Mein Kampf* from a prison
ll. In the book he detailed his plans for re-
ring Germany to glory. He believed the Ger-
an Aryans were a master race of people. That
ster race did not include Jews.

B. Japan invaded Manchuria in northern
ina in 1931. Many historians consider this
be the beginning of World War II.

A. Pearl Harbor was attacked on December
1941. The United States entered World War
in both Europe and the Pacific shortly after.

6. **D.** German blitzkrieg of Poland, 1939;
France falls to Hitler, 1940; Japan attacks Pearl
Harbor, 1941; Dropping of the Atomic Bomb
on Hiroshima, 1945.

7. **A.** D-Day, or the Invasion of Normandy, was
June 6, 1944. It led to the liberation of France,
and the eventual surrender of the Nazis less
than one year later.

8. **B.** Stalin received much of Eastern Europe
at the Yalta Conference. Although he promised
free elections, nations of Eastern Europe became satellites of the Soviet Union.

9. **A.** The Nuremberg laws were passed in 1935.
They denied Jews basic rights within Germany.

10. **C.** Elie Wiesel wrote *Night*, in which he
detailed his survival of the Holocaust. Primary
sources from Wiesel, Anne Frank, and other
victims and survivors have brought to light the
tragedy of the Holocaust.

The Cold War, and Wars in Korea and Vietnam

After World War II, the United States and Soviet Union remained the only superpowers in the world. Although the two countries never directly fought, they antagonized each other throughout the Cold War. A space race, blockade of Berlin, spy plane controversy, and near nuclear war over Cuba were just some of the issues during these tense decades. The two fought "puppet wars," as America's policy to contain communism led them to conflicts in both Korea and Vietnam.

HERE IS WHAT YOU NEED TO KNOW:

• THE COLD WAR

Question: Why was it called a Cold War?

Answer: No, it's not because it's cold in Russia. The Cold War was fought (or not fought) between the US and the Soviet Union from 1945-1991. Although they never directly attacked one another, there were puppet wars at times, like Korea and Vietnam. One could argue that it's called a Cold War because bullets are hot and none were directly fired at each other. You might also say that the US and Soviet Union displayed cold feelings towards one another.

Question: What were the differences between the US and USSR?

Answer:

United States = Political system is democracy, and economic system is capitalism.

Soviet Union = Political system was dictatorship, and economic system was socialism. Dictatorship + Socialism = Communism.

The US wanted to: 1) contain communism, 2) rebuild Eastern Europe to provide the US with new markets for products, and 3) reunite Germany.

The Soviet Union wanted to: 1) spread communism, 2) control Eastern Europe to protect Soviet borders, and 3) keep Germany divided.

Definition: Containment

The foreign policy of the United States during the Cold War was containment. US diplomat George Kennan coined this term that meant preventing the spread of communism. This was typically done by forming alliances with weaker countries to fend off communist aggression. Containment is the opposite of appeasement (giving in to what the aggressor wants). Containment is also the most important term of the Cold War. Why did the US get involved in Korea? Containment. Why did the US send troops to Vietnam? Containment. Why did the US spend so much money on the military? Containment.

Definition: Truman Doctrine and Marshall Plan, 1947

The Doctrine gave military aid (no troops) to countries resisting communism. Greece and Turkey took advantage of the aid.

US Secretary of State George Marshall's plan was a strategy to give economic aid to countries that were not communist. The idea was to make countries stronger, and less susceptible to communist takeovers. About $12 billion was given to nations all over Europe.

Definition: Berlin Airlift, 1948

Soviet leader Joseph Stalin, wanting to keep Germany divided, blockaded the highway and rail resources coming into West Berlin (the non-communist side). He hoped this would make West Berlin dependent upon him and his satellites for supplies. However, the US and

eat Britain sent 277,000 flights full of food
d necessities for the German people. A furi-
s Stalin thought the airlift might lead to war
th the US. But, as with everything else in the
ld War, direct conflict was avoided.

Definition: NATO vs. Warsaw Pact

Think of these two as the gangs of the Cold
ar. NATO (North Atlantic Treaty Organiza-
n) was founded in 1949 and supported de-
ocracy. The Warsaw Pact, consisting of the
viet Union and their satellites, was founded
1955 and was referred to more commonly as
e Communist Bloc.

Definition: Sputnik, 1957

In 1957, the Soviets successfully launched
satellite named Sputnik into space. Not only
d this make Americans nervous about Soviet
chnology, but it gave the US a feeling of in-
riority. The result of Sputnik's launch was an
merican increase of spending on education
d science. In 1969, the US would win the
ace race to the moon.

Definition: U-2, 1960

It's not the rock band. But, if you look at
me of their cover art, you will see a plane.
e U-2 was a spy plane that was shot out of
e Soviet sky in 1960. Although the US de-
ed a spy plane was flying behind the iron cur-
in (metaphor for Soviet border), the evidence
as clear. Francis Gary Powers, the pilot, was
ld captive. The incident proved that distrust
etween the superpowers was real, and other
ies were likely attempting to infiltrate both
rders.

Definition: H-Bomb

The H-Bomb, or Hydrogen Bomb, worked
fusion. It was 1,000 times more powerful
an the Atomic Bomb that worked on fission.

The fear of a nuclear war was the underlying
story of the Cold War, as it led to "duck and
cover" drills in the US, as well as the creation
of bomb shelters.

Definition: Brinkmanship

This meant going to the brink of war, but
coming just short of fighting. The escalation of
brinkmanship peaked from 1961-1962.

Definition: Berlin Wall

In 1961, Nikita Khrushchev's Soviet Union
built the wall that would formally divide communist East Berlin from non-communist West
Berlin. President John F. Kennedy traveled
to the wall to deliver his famous *Ich Bin Ein
Berliner* (I am a Berliner) speech. He told the
people of Berlin that the rest of the world was
behind them. It is disputed that what Kennedy said translated to "I am a doughnut" in the
speech (a Berliner is also a jelly doughnut). In
1987 President Ronald Reagan traveled to Berlin to give his famous, "tear down this wall"
speech as a challenge to Soviet leader Mikhail
Gorbachev. The wall came down in 1989.

Definition: Bay of Pigs Invasion, April 17, 1961

Fidel Castro, a communist, took over Cuba
in 1959. Having a communist country just
90 miles from the United States was a scary
thought for most Americans. President John F.
Kennedy wanted to get rid of any nearby communist influence. The US supported a rebellion
led by Cuban exiles. They were defeated at the
Bay of Pigs in Cuba. Not only did the US sponsor the failed rebellion, but the event strengthened the legitimacy of Castro.

Definition: Cuban Missile Crisis, October of 1962

The closest the United States and Soviet

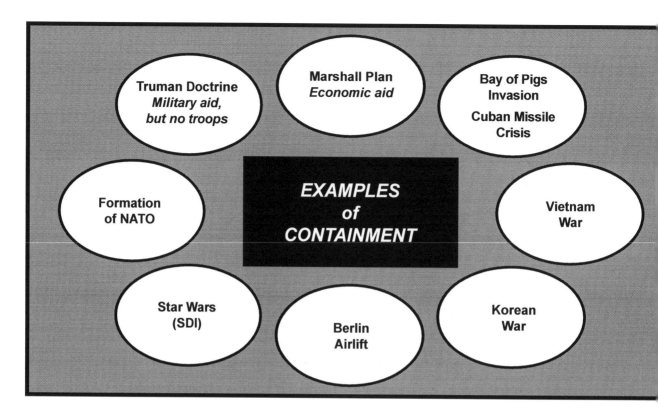

Union ever came to nuclear war was during these two weeks of October. After the Bay of Pigs Invasion, Cuban and Soviet relations were quite good. So good, in fact, that the Soviets moved enough missiles to Cuba to destroy American cities. When US intelligence learned of this, Kennedy took it as a threat of war. His solution was to:

1. Blockade (quarantine) Cuba by surrounding it with US naval ships. The goal was to prevent the delivery of Soviet weapons.

2. Threaten force if Khrushchev did not remove the missiles.

Ultimately, cooler heads prevailed, and Khrushchev removed the missiles. In return, the US agreed not to invade Cuba. Furthermore, the US removed missiles of their own from Turkey.

Definition: Détente

This means an easing of Cold War tensions. The Cuban Missile Crisis scared the heck out of everyone. The 1970s had friendlier diplomacy between the two superpowers. President Ric ard Nixon and Soviet leader Leonid Brezhn were sometimes seen smiling together. The k détente event to know is:

SALT - Strategic Arms Limitation Tal This was a treaty in 1972 that limited the nu ber of nuclear weapons each country had their arsenal. Of course, this was all a charac as no one knew for sure how many weapo each country had stockpiled.

Definition: Soviet-Afghanistan War

Afghanistan bordered the Soviet Union. 1979, the Soviets invaded and attempted take over the country. However, strong Afgh resistance, and United States aid to the Afgh people, prevented a permanent takeover. T Soviets withdrew in 1989.

Definition: Star Wars/Strategic Defense In tiative

President Ronald Reagan abandoned d

Soldiers step out of their tanks, signaling the end of communist rule in the Soviet Union

nte. Strategic Defense Initiative was an elaborate technological endeavor that looked to zap issiles out of the sky. The plan sounded like ience fiction, so it was labeled *Star Wars*.

uestion: How did communism ultimately ll?

Answer: With ***Mikhail Gorbachev's*** rule ver the Soviet Union there was a new outlook. fter he took office in 1985, the Soviet Union lopted two major policies:

1. *Glasnost* - this meant an *openness* that alwed people to voice their views on government.

2. *Perestroika* - this was a restructuring of conomics, including some private business wnership.

By 1991, Communism was falling all over Europe. Gorbachev lost his legitimacy, as the people supported a member of parliament named Boris Yeltsin to be their new president. In a desperate action to keep the Soviet Union in Communist Party hands, the conservative *State Committee* detained Gorbachev and ordered the military to attack the parliament. This ***August Coup*** (August 19-21, 1991) failed when soldiers stepped out of their tanks and refused to fight for the Communist conspirators. Gorbachev later resigned, and Yeltsin became president. The Soviet Union dissolved into the CIS, or Commonwealth of Independent States. Soon after, Russia became a country again.

Question: In what other European nations did communism fall?

Answer: Note: China, Cuba, and Vietnam

continued to be communist. In Europe:

1. In 1990, East and West Germany came together in a process called ***reunification***. The Berlin Wall came down.

2. With the economy weakening, Poland, with help from ***Lech Walesa*** and his labor union ***Solidarity***, was able to get free elections in 1989. Soon after, Poland was free from communist rule.

3. In 1989, a rather peaceful student protest in Czechoslovakia, known as the ***Velvet Revolution***, began in Prague and spread to the rest of the country. Years earlier in 1968, a movement for free speech and democratic reform was put down by Warsaw Pact troops in an event known as the ***Prague Spring***. However, the Velvet Revolution was successful in eliminating communist rule. In 1993, Czechoslovakia became two nations, The Czech Republic and Slovakia.

4. Yugoslavia experienced bloody conflict as it broke apart. With different ethnic groups in the area, there was a struggle for territory. In Bosnia-Herzegovina, ***ethnic cleansing***, or the violent elimination of a group from an area, occurred as Serbs attempted to remove Muslim influences from Bosnia. Ethnic cleansing involved executions and other human rights violations. The term "ethnic cleansing" is used because the atrocities were done as a war measure to remove people. Nonetheless, many consider the killings to be genocide. In 1995, NATO forces began a bombing campaign to control the conflict.

• KOREAN AND VIETNAM WARS
Question: What do I need to know about the Korean War?
Answer:

The UN voted to send troops into the area after communist North Korea crossed the 38th parallel and attacked non-communist South Korea in 1950. At that time, Taiwan (Republic of China), not the communist People's Republic of China, was recognized as a permanent nation of the UN. Communist China would have blocked the deployment of troops. In protest, the Soviet Union abstained from the vote. Therefore, no one vetoed the deployment of UN troops to stop the spread of communism in Korea.

The war ended in 1953 leaving an estimated death toll in the millions. In the aftermath, massive American aid poured into South Korea for decades. The 38th parallel is still the dividing line in Korea today, as the two countries are buffered by a demilitarized zone (DMZ).

Definition: Domino Theory

This was a belief in the United States that if one nation in Asia fell to communism, then the rest of the nations would also fall...like dominos. It was important to stop that first country from becoming communist. (See chart on next page.)

Definition: Dien Bien Phu and Gulf of Tonkin Resolution

In 1954, the French saw the city of Dien Bien Phu fall to the communists and their leader, ***Ho Chi Minh***. Minh used nationalism as a unifying force to drive out the French and spread communism. Under Presidents Dwight Eisenhower and John F. Kennedy, there was a gradual escalation of a US military presence in Southern Vietnam. When President Kennedy was assassinated in 1963, Vice President Lyndon B. Johnson became President.

In 1964, at the Gulf of Tonkin in Vietnam, American ships were fired on (the severity of this was likely embellished). After the event, Congress approved the Resolution which gave Johnson a "blank check" to use the military as he saw fit in Vietnam. This meant a large escalation of American forces.

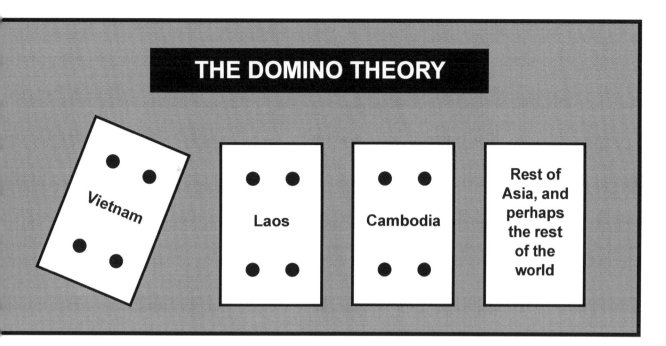

THE DOMINO THEORY

Vietnam | Laos | Cambodia | Rest of Asia, and perhaps the rest of the world

Definition: Vietcong

The Vietcong were communist guerilla soldiers in *South* Vietnam. Vietnam was divided at the 17th parallel. As with Korea, the communists were supposed to be in the North...not the South.

Question: Militarily, what do I need to know about the Vietnam War?

Answer:

1. Much of the war was fought on dangerous terrain in a jungle.

2. Napalm was an explosive chemical that was used extensively in Vietnam. Agent Orange was a chemical used by the United States to remove leaves from the trees where guerilla soldiers were positioned. Years later, this chemical was known to cause cancer to many American Vietnam veterans.

3. The Tet (lunar New Year) Offensive of 1968 was a massive thrust southward by the communists in the North. Although the United States pushed back the attack, the battle had a catastrophic affect on American morale, while increasing support for the communists within Vietnam.

4. In 1973, President Richard Nixon pulled American troops out of Vietnam. The country became communist shortly thereafter.

Definition: Vietnamization

Richard Nixon's plan to *gradually remove US troops* from Vietnam was called Vietnamization. He hoped to turn the war over to Vietnamese soldiers. As stated above, the US pulled out for good in 1973.

Definition: Khmer Rouge

When the United States pulled out of Vietnam, the country turned communist. Communism spread to neighboring Cambodia. In 1975 a group called the Khmer Rouge set up a government under their leader *Pol Pot*. Under his reign (1975-1979) more than 2 million Cambodians were killed through forced labor or execution. The sites of the atrocities are commonly referred to as the *Killing Fields*.

Definition: Aung San Suu Kyi

In neighboring Myanmar (formerly called Burma), the military ruled as a dictatorship.

Aung San Suu Kyi was instrumental in a non-violent protest movement for democracy and human rights. Despite winning the 1991 Nobel Peace Prize, she spent over a decade as a political prisoner. After being freed in 2010, she won a parliament seat in 2012.

Question: How did Southeast Asia gain autonomy?

Answer: After the Age of Imperialism, Southeast Asia was controlled by European nations. However, as imperialism became expensive and unpopular, countries gained their own rule (autonomy).

1. The United States fought to control the Philippines in a bloody conflict c1900. The Philippines gained their independence in 1946. Ferdinand Marcos is a leader you should know. He stole from the people, and was exiled a[fter] he refused to accept the results of an elect[ion] he lost in 1986.

2. Indonesia is a complex network of [is]lands in the Pacific. It is one of the most c[ul]turally diverse places in the world. Indo[ne]sia was controlled by the Dutch, and then [the] Japanese. Sukarno was the leader of the Ind[o]nesian independence movement. After W[orld] War II, he declared the region independe[nt]. Despite a Dutch attempt to regain the te[rri]tory, Indonesia was officially granted in[de]pendence by the Netherlands in 1949. Un[der] the dictator Suharto, Indonesia was ruled [by] the military, and many suspected communi[sts] were executed.

In the twenty-first century, the most practi[ced] religion in Southeast Asia has become Islam[.]

The United States policy of containment
cant
A) appeasement to the Soviet Union
B) an attack on the Soviet Union and its satellites
C) the division of Germany into zones controlled by the West and Soviet Union
D) stopping both the spread of communism and Soviet Union interests

The Truman Doctrine
A) offered combat troops to help countries fighting communism
B) gave economic aid to scientists developing the H-Bomb
C) provided military aid, but not troops, to foreign countries threatened by communism
D) looked to expand democracy to areas in the Middle East

What was John F. Kennedy's main course of tion during the Cuban Missile Crisis?
A) A threat of force and a strict quarantine of Cuba
B) A calculated invasion of the Cuban mainland at the Bay of Pigs
C) Diplomacy with Nikita Khrushchev which led to the disarmament of missiles in exchange for American bases in the Caribbean
D) A treaty with the Cubans which transferred the missiles to Poland

4. Détente is most associated with
A) The Marshall Plan
B) The Truman Doctrine
C) Strategic Arms Limitation Talks
D) The Vietnam War

5. After the Korean War, South Korea
A) isolated itself to Western markets
B) battled communist invaders from the south
C) suffered decades of oppressive rule
D) industrialized with the help of American aid

6. Why was the Tet Offensive significant?
A) It led to a takeover of South Vietnam by the Vietcong
B) When the Northern Vietnamese moved south, it decreased the morale of American forces
C) It was the deciding battle in the American victory over the communists in Vietnam
D) Ho Chi Minh's proclamation of victory led to an American withdrawal of troops

7. The Gulf of Tonkin Resolution
A) hastened the policy of Vietnamization
B) allowed President Nixon to pull out of Vietnam
C) led to the escalation of the War in Vietnam
D) denied due process of law to Vietcong prisoners

8. All of the following occurred as part of the Fall of Communism in Europe EXCEPT:
A) Velvet Revolution
B) Reunification of Germany
C) August Coup
D) Prague Spring

9. Glasnost and perestroika were policies that looked to

A) stop the spread of communism in Southeast Asia

B) open the Soviet Union to criticism and capitalism

C) spread communism to markets in Eastern Europe

D) send United Nations troops to South Vietnam

10. Lech Walesa acted to

A) bring more rights to the workers of Poland

B) economically restructure the Soviet Union

C) replace Michael Gorbachev as the leader of the Soviet Union

D) strengthen the grip of communism in Eastern Europe

D. Containment meant to stop the spread of mmunism. That was the main objective of nerican Cold War policies.

C. Greece and Turkey took advantage of the uman Doctrine's military aid.

A. Kennedy threatened an invasion of Cuba er a strict quarantine. Khrushchev removed e missiles from Cuba, and the United States sarmed some of theirs in Turkey.

C. Détente meant a lessening of Cold War nsions. SALT was a treaty that limited nucle- missiles in both the United States and Soviet nion.

D. After the Korean War, massive American d helped South Korea industrialize. They be- me a strong trading partner, and a nation less sceptible to a communist takeover.

B. The Tet Offensive was when the North ietnamese pushed South. This led to a de- ease in American morale.

7. **C**. The Gulf of Tonkin Resolution gave President Johnson a "blank check" for dealing with the military crisis in Vietnam.

8. **D**. The Prague Spring was in 1968, well before the Fall of Communism. Although reforms were demanded, the movement was put down by the Warsaw Pact. The other choices reflect the Fall of Communism in modern-day Czech Republic, East Germany, and the Soviet Union.

9. **B**. Glasnost brought a feeling of openness to the historically rigid rule of the Communist Party in the Soviet Union. Perestroika looked to economically restructure the nation.

10. **A**. Lech Walesa was the leader of the Polish labor union, Solidarity. He helped weaken communist domination in Poland and gave workers more rights.

China and India After 1900

China and India were great imperial treasures of Britain in the nineteenth century. By the twentieth century, they both longed to expel foreigners and gain independence. In China, the overthrow of their Emperor was sparked by hopes for democracy. However, during the twentieth century China experienced Japanese imperialism, followed by the firm hand of dictatorship and communism. Despite civil war and adversity, China turned into an industrial giant at the brink of the twenty-first century. India also grew industrially after shaking off imperial rule. With hopes for independence, Mohandas Gandhi became an inspirational leader. Through passive resistance and civil disobedience, Gandhi and his followers gained support from around the world. However, after receiving independence in 1947, the region has experienced intense religious conflict and threats of war.

HERE IS WHAT YOU NEED TO KNOW:

• CHINA
Definition: Sun Yixian (Sun Yat-sen) and Qing Overthrow

The Qing (Manchu) was the last dynasty of China. In 1911, Dr. Sun Yixian of the Kuomintang (political party known as the Nationalist Party) helped overthrow the emperor. Yixian promised *Three Principles of the Chinese People*. They were:

1. Nationalism/People's Rule - This meant to bring unity and pride to the Chinese people who had been imperialized by foreign nations for almost a century.

2. Democracy - A goal of creating a government that met the needs of the people and ensured rights.

3. People's Livelihood - Making sure that everyone had a comfortable standard of living.

Though bold, Yixian never could unify the people, and civil unrest continued in China.

Definition: May Fourth Movement

After Japan received more land in China after World War I, young Chinese students took to the streets in protest. Demonstrations reached their peak on May 4, 1919, as a widespread nationalistic movement protested Japanese occupation. Many of these protesters would soon support a new form of government…communism.

Definition: Mao Zedong (Mao Tse-tung)

Mao Zedong took part in the demonstrations against Japan. He was also one of the founders of the Communist Party in China. Eventually, communists became influential in the Kuomintang. When Yixian died, a dictator named *Jiang Jieshi (Chiang Kai-shek)* took over. He was anti-communist, and ordered the execution of many of their supporters. Despite the decrease in numbers within the government, communist popularity grew under Mao, and the seeds for a takeover were planted.

Question: Why did people turn to communism in China?

Answer:

1. Anti-imperialistic sentiment, notably against Japan. People wanted new leadership that could drive them out.

2. Communism seemed to be working in the Soviet Union. The Soviet Union had close ties to communists in China.

3. Communists promised land reform and equality to starving peasants.

4. By 1930, Jiang Jieshi's government was

Mao's picture marks the spot in Tiananmen Square where he founded the People's Republic of China in 1949

npopular and abusing its power.

As seen in the Soviet Union, Mao offered an increase in women's rights. This meant marriage rights and an end to being publicly subservient. After he secured power, women were expected to provide for the state as well as their families.

Definition: Chinese Civil War 1927-1949

Jiang Jieshi's Nationalists fought *Mao Zedong's Communists*. You need to know:

1. It seemed that by 1934 the Communists were all but defeated. However, Mao Zedong went on a 6,000 mile trek known as the *Long March*. As he paraded around the country, he avoided capture and gathered supporters. The longer the war went on, the better it was for Mao.

2. The Japanese invaded Manchuria (northern China) in 1931, thereby starting World War in Asia. They were attracted to the area be-

cause of an abundance of raw materials such as coal and iron. By the late 1930s, they had a stronghold in China. This forced Jieshi and Mao to agree on a ceasefire, thereby becoming reluctant allies against Japan.

3. After World War II, the civil war continued. The United States gave aid to the Nationalists, while the Soviets supported the Communists.

4. In 1949 the Communists claimed victory, and on October 1, 1949, Mao declared China's new name to be the *People's Republic of China*. The Nationalists and Jiang Jieshi fled to the island of Taiwan. The United Nations recognized Taiwan as the Republic of China until 1971. That year, the People's Republic of China was seated.

Definition: The Great Leap Forward, 1958-1961

This was Mao's plan to develop agriculture

113

and industry. People were forced to live with other families on large plots of land called *communes*. Here, they collectively worked together. Citizens were encouraged to create furnaces in their backyards to make steel materials. Despite the increase in production, the Great Leap Forward was mostly a failure because bad weather and depleted agricultural workforces led to poor harvests and famines that killed millions. Furthermore, there was an overproduction of shoddy finished goods.

Definition: Cultural Revolution, 1966-1976

In the Cultural Revolution, Mao's government unleashed a massive censorship campaign that targeted intellectuals or any who dissented with the rule of the Communist Party. Chinese citizens were instructed to carry a Little Red Book entitled *Quotations from Chairman Mao*, which contained his famous speeches and thoughts.

Before the Cultural Revolution, Mao encouraged intellectuals to criticize his government when he said "let a hundred flowers bloom, let a hundred schools of thought contend." However, he didn't like the harsh criticism.

In the Cultural Revolution, many were killed or forced to do hard labor. The Cultural Revolution began in 1966, and ended with Mao Zedong's death in 1976.

Definition: Deng Xiaoping and the Four Modernizations

Today, China is one of the leading industrial powers in the world. However until about 1980, it lagged behind most other nations. Deng Xiaoping helped get the ball rolling on massive industrialization with a program called the *Four Modernizations*. Inheriting this policy from a decade before, he set new goals for agriculture, industry, and technology. Small businesses were permitted to operate,

China's modernization can be felt in every aspect of society even in the bathrooms

and with their profits, people began to purcha consumer goods. By the twenty-first centur China became an industrial giant, and the fas est growing economy in the world c2000.

Definition: Tiananmen Square Massacr 1989

Although China has welcomed industri ization and modified capitalism, they remain communist nation. In 1989, students proteste communist rule and peacefully campaign for democracy in Beijing's Tiananmen Squar Deng Xiaoping's soldiers opened fire, killin many protesters. Although the massacre w condemned by nations around the world, der onstrations in China were quickly silence There's a famous photograph associated wi the tragedy where a protester stands in front a moving tank. The media labeled this pers "Tank Man." Estimates of the dead and woun ed exceed 2,000.

Definition: Tibet Independence Movemen

Once an independent country, Tibet is a r gion in western China. The People's Republ of China took over the area in the early 195(but promised autonomy to the Tibetans a their religious leader, the Dalai Lama. Ho ver, Tibet never gained self-rule. Through e years, several uprisings have led to deportions. The Tibetans cite human rights violaons. The Chinese government denies these aims. Despite international pressure, Tibet mains part of China.

efinition: Pollution and One-Child Policy, 978

China continues to grow at an incredible te. Huge building projects, such as the *Three orges Dam* (mostly operational by 2008) n the Yangtze River, surpassed other similar orldwide constructions. China's speedy inustrialization has been accompanied by imense pollution. It has led nations and sciensts to criticize China's environmental policies. China's population is well over 1 billion. earful of running out of resources, the governent instituted the One-Child Policy in 1978. his *family planning policy* limited much of e population (mostly city dwellers) to proicing only one offspring.

INDIA

uestion: How did World War I coincide ith Indian demands for independence?

Answer: British-Indian troops served proudin World War I. However, this did not lead India's independence from Britain. Outrage ver imperial occupation in India grew by 919, and protests emerged all over the couny. Notably, a peaceful demonstration turned eadly in Amritsar, Punjab.

efinition: Rowlatt Act/Amritsar Massacre, 919

The *Rowlatt Act* was passed at the end of orld War I to control political unrest and poential terrorist threats to British rule in India. he law allowed British officials to round up spected activists and imprison them without

a trial. Furthermore, free speech and assembly were outlawed. When a group of Hindus and Muslims assembled in the city of Amritsar to give political speeches, British officer Reginald Dyer ordered his troops to fire. Hundreds were killed, and almost 1,500 were wounded. The massacre led to immense anti-British sentiment amongst the Indian people.

Definition: Mohandas K. Gandhi

Gandhi led a push for Indian independence from the British crown. His methods and education combined both Western and Eastern thought. Gandhi preached *civil disobedience* (disobeying laws seen as unjust) and *passive resistance* (peaceful protest). Resistance was achieved through powerful boycotts of British finished goods (specifically spun goods), refusal to pay taxes, and lack of government participation. Known also for his hunger strikes, Gandhi's most famous act of disobedience involved salt (explained next).

Definition: Salt March, 1930

The Indian people were forced to purchase salt from the *British Raj* (name for British rule). This salt was taxed. Gandhi and his followers protested this British monopoly by marching 240 miles to the coastal city of Dandi to get their own salt. As the movement for salt escalated, British authorities violently beat the protesters. When the Western media got wind of the British oppression, Gandhi gained international support. India received gradual gains for independence in the mid 1930s, and total independence in 1947.

Definition: Partition, 1947

India's fight for independence from Britain gave way to an internal struggle among religions. When Britain withdrew from India in 1947, the country was divided (partitioned) into the independent nations of:

1. India - Which was mostly comprised of Hindus who were supported by the Indian National Congress.

2. Pakistan - Which was mostly comprised of Muslims who were supported by the Muslim League. Their early leader was *Muhammad Ali Jinnah*.

Gandhi tried to bring peace between the region's Hindus, Muslims, and Sikhs (a monotheistic religion popular in Punjab, India). However in 1948, he was assassinated by a Hindu extremist who was upset that Gandhi was negotiating with Muslims. Violence after partition was fierce. There is still animosity between these two nuclear nations today, especially on the border in the disputed region of *Kashmir*.

Question: What later happened in this region?

Answer:

1. *Jawaharlal Nehru* became prime minster of India for two decades. He supported democracy and westernization. His daughter *Indira Gandhi* also became prime minister. Religious conflict and terrorism plagued the nation. Both Gandhi and her son Rajiv Gandhi were assassinated (1984, 1991).

2. Political strife also affected Pakistan. Originally, there was West and East Pakistan. However, the distance between the two regions created a split in culture and political decision making. East Pakistan became *Bangladesh*.

3. In Pakistan, *Benazir Bhutto* became first woman ever to lead a Muslim state. After facing corruption charges, she exiled herself 1998. She returned in 2007, and was assassinated as she campaigned for public office.

4. In Sri Lanka, a militant separatist group from Southern India, known as the *Tamil Tigers*, fought for a homeland in Buddhist Sri Lanka. From 1983-2009 there was a civil war. The Tamil Tigers engaged in guerilla military and terror activities. They never gained a homeland in Sri Lanka.

5. Today, India is one of the fastest growing economies in the world. However, there is a wide gap between the rich and the poor. With its population over a billion, parts of India remain incredibly impoverished. India has moved towards democracy over the last few decades. However, the presence of the caste system prevents total democracy from taking place.

Sun Yixian hoped to bring which of the following to China?
A) Communist rule
B) The beginnings of democracy
C) Division of farmland amongst the peasants
D) A restoration of the Emperor

Mao Zedong's Long March resulted in which the following in the 1930s?
A) Recruitment of more communist allies from within China
B) The disappearance of Japanese imperialism
C) The deportation of Jiang Jieshi
D) An unconditional surrender of communist forces

The creation of communes and an increased oduction of finished goods by local families most associated with
A) The Cultural Revolution
B) The Four Modernizations
C) The Great Leap Forward
D) The May Fourth Movement

The Four Modernizations could be considered the inspiration for the
A) One-Child Policy
B) Three Gorges Dam
C) Cultural Revolution
D) Great Leap Forward

5. The Cultural Revolution attempted to
A) incorporate Western thought and philosophy
B) encourage free speech and expression
C) bring great wealth to individual landlords
D) contain opposition to the Communist Party

6. The Tiananmen Square and Amritsar massacres directly resulted in
A) more violent protests against China's Communist Party and the British Raj
B) civil rights being bestowed on the peasants of China and India
C) international outrage and pressures for reform
D) the Fall of Communism in China, and end to British rule in India

7. All of the following were tactics used by Mohandas Gandhi EXCEPT:
A) Boycott of British taxes
B) Hunger strikes
C) Segregation of Hindus and Muslims
D) Passive resistance

8. An example of civil disobedience was the
A) Salt March
B) creation of the state of Bangladesh
C) partition of India
D) formation of the Muslim League

9. After the British pulled out of the region, why was there still conflict in India?

A) There was anti-imperialistic sentiment against the United States

B) Religious strife escalated between Hindus and Muslims

C) There were political conflicts between India and China

D) The increased price of salt led to economic distress

10. The Tamil Tigers attempted to gain a hor land in Sri Lanka through

A) civil disobedience

B) guerilla military tactics

C) passive resistance

D) an alliance with Pakistan

Answers and Explanations

B. Sun Yixian's *Three Principles of the Chinese People* looked to bring democratic reforms, a fair standard of living, and the elimination of imperialism.

A. Mao Zedong went on a 6,000 mile march through China to avoid the Nationalist military and Jiang Jieshi. During the march, the communists recruited many supporters.

C. The Great Leap Forward is considered to be a failure by historians. It looked to increase production and agricultural output at local levels.

B. The Four Modernizations looked to increase industry and technology in China. When it became fully operational in 2008, the Three Gorges Dam became the largest hydro-electric dam in the world.

D. Mao ruled harshly during the Cultural Revolution. During this time, opposition to the Communist Party was severely punished.

6. **C.** Both incidents led to international outrage. Because it occurred more recently, images of the Tiananmen Square Massacre of 1989 were seen all over the world.

7. **C.** Although there was much religious strife between Hindus and Muslims within the region, Gandhi embraced all religions.

8. **A.** Gandhi led the Salt March in 1930 to defy the British salt monopoly. Gandhi and his followers hoped to secure their own salt.

9. **B.** The end of the British Raj led to new problems in the area between Hindus and Muslims. In 1947, the country was partitioned into Pakistan, a predominantly Muslim state, and India, a mostly Hindu one. Much violence took place on the border in the disputed region of Kashmir.

10. **B.** The Tamil Tigers were a guerilla military organization that used terror tactics.

Post World War II Middle East, Africa, and the Modern World

Since World War II, the Middle East has been in constant conflict. After gaining independence, Israel fought wars in the first four decades of its existence. Despite attempts for diplomacy, violence in the Middle East continued into the twenty-first century. In Africa, some nations received independence after nearly a century of imperialism. However, conflict and violence still plagued the area, as feuding tribes and religions resulted in wars and massacres. In South Africa, decades of segregation and oppression finally ended in the 1990s, as apartheid dissolved. The world has changed a lot since the Neolithic Revolution. Today, interdependent nations deal with problems such as pollution, economic crashes, and environmental destruction. All of these issues have left many concerned about the future.

HERE IS WHAT YOU NEED TO KNOW:

• THE MIDDLE EAST
Definition: Zionism

Led by Theodor Herzl, this was a movement in the late nineteenth century to find a permanent homeland for Jews in the Holy Land of the Middle East. In 1917, a letter (known as the *Balfour Declaration*) written by British Foreign Secretary Arthur James Balfour called for the creation of a Jewish state within Palestine of the Middle East.

After suffering through the Holocaust, Jews received a homeland when the United Nations recommended the creation of a Jewish state in 1947. Israel gained independence on May 14, 1948. Almost immediately, Arab nations invaded in what would become the first of four Arab-Israeli wars. Israel pushed back this early threat. David Ben-Gurion became the first Prime Minister of Israel.

Question: What wars were fought between Israel and other Middle East nations from 1956-1973?

Answer: After the initial 1948 conflict, the following occurred:

1. Suez Crisis, 1956 - The Suez Canal wa completed in 1869, and controlled by Eure pean nations as a means to connect the Re Sea to the Mediterranean Sea. Egypt's leade *Gamal Abdel Nasser*, took control of the can in 1956. This angered Britain and France, wh aligned with Israel to take it back. Despite the military victory, international pressure fro the US and Soviet Union led to the withdraw of troops from the area.

2. Six-Day War, 1967 - Egypt threatene war with Israel. In response, Israel made pr emptive strikes against Egypt and neighborir Arab nations. After the war, Israel controlle Jerusalem, the Sinai Peninsula, and the We Bank.

3. Yom-Kippur War, 1973 - Led by Egy and Syria, Arab nations surprised Israel on tl holiest day of the Jewish calendar, Yom Ki pur. They caused heavy losses and gained son land. Israel took back much of it before a ceas fire. During the 1970s, Israel received much a from the United States through the diploma of their Prime Minister, *Golda Meir*. She w one of the Zionists influential in the creation the State of Israel.

Definition: Camp David Accords, 1978

This was one of the rare peace agreemer in the Middle East. Menachem Begin of Isra Anwar Sadat of Egypt, and President Jimm Carter of the United States met at Camp Dav in Maryland. There, it was agreed that Egy would recognize Israel as a nation-state, ar

Israel would give back the Sinai Peninsula. Diplomacy with Israel angered many Muslims, and Sadat (like Gandhi) was assassinated by an extremist of his own faith.

Definition: Iranian Revolution, 1979

In 1978, anti-Western riots spread throughout Iran. To control order, *martial law* (emergency military rule) was established by Western ally Mohammad Reza Pahlavi - the Shah of Iran. Still, opposition mounted. As his popularity decreased, the Shah fled Iran and *Ayatollah Khomeini* took power in 1979. Khomeini supported an Islamic state, not a westernized one.

That same year, Iranian students stormed the US Embassy in Tehran. For 444 days, Americans were held hostage.

Question: What other violence occurred in the area?

Answer: Israel, Jordan, and Egypt coexisted rather peacefully in the late twentieth and early twenty-first centuries. However, violence between Israelis and Palestinians continued. In the 1970s, the *PLO* (Palestine Liberation Organization) was led by *Yasser Arafat*. Arafat hoped to get self-determination for a Palestinian State. Much violence occurred in the area. In 1993 President Bill Clinton attempted to bring peace between Arafat and Israeli Prime Minister *Yitzhak Rabin*. Israel agreed to withdraw some troops and permit Palestinians to self-govern the territories of the Gaza Strip and West Bank. Rabin, like Sadat, was killed by an extremist of his own faith who thought the Prime Minister negotiated too much.

In 2007, the political group Hamas took power in Gaza. In 2008, Israel blockaded the Gaza Strip when rockets were being fired at them. This escalated into the Gaza-Israeli War. Israel issued a ceasefire less than a month after invading, as worldwide criticism of occupation increased. A similar war took place a year before, as rockets came from the north from an organization called Hezbollah in Lebanon. After 34 days of fighting, the UN negotiated a ceasefire.

In 2011, the Middle East saw a wave of democratic protests and reforms, most notably in Egypt where President Hosni Mubarak was removed from power. From 2011-12, violent protests spread to Syria, where leader President Bashar al-Assad responded with military force. He was accused of crimes against humanity.

Definition: OPEC

The Organization of Petroleum Exporting Countries is a very influential union of the world's largest oil producing nations such as Iran, Saudi Arabia, and Venezuela. They control the production of much of the globe's crude oil supply. Therefore, they have great influence on the worldwide prices of oil and gasoline products.

Definition: Taliban

The Taliban controlled a *fundamentalist* (strict adherence to religious principles) Islamic government in Afghanistan c2000. They isolated themselves from most of the Western World. The Taliban supported the terrorist organization al Qaeda, which was behind the attacks on the United States on September 11, 2001. Osama bin Laden organized the crashing of hijacked planes into New York's World Trade Center, and the Pentagon in Washington, DC. A final plane crashed in an open field in Pennsylvania after heroic actions by passengers.

The United States went to war with the Taliban in 2001, and quickly removed them from power. In 2003, the US invaded Saddam Hussein's Iraq. Hussein was captured in 2003, and later tried for crimes against humanity. He was executed in 2006. The United States spent more than a decade in Afghanistan and Iraq reconstructing the war-torn countries.

• AFRICA
Definition: Apartheid in South Africa, 1948-1994

Given self-rule from Great Britain, the Republic of South Africa's white National Party members and Afrikaners (Dutch descendants) discriminated against black Africans. *Apartheid* (notice the word apart) was a separation of the *majority* black population from the *minority* white race in South Africa. The entire country was segregated for nearly 50 years.

Definition: Nelson Mandela

Black South Africans protested apartheid, and formed the *African National Congress*. The ANC supported boycotts and strikes to bring attention to apartheid. The government cracked down on this organization's activities and imprisoned many followers. One man arrested was *Nelson Mandela*. Mandela became a symbol of the resistance movement, as he sat in a prison cell from 1962-1990. Explained next, he was instrumental in bringing an end to apartheid. He was awarded the Nobel Peace Prize in 1993.

Question: How did apartheid end?

Answer: Sympathizing with protests in South Africa, the world rallied against apartheid. A bishop named *Desmond Tutu* helped bring attention to the injustice, and gathered support against it. Countries leveled sanctions (economic punishments) and trade embargos on South Africa. In 1990 F.W. de Klerk, the new President of South Africa, released Mandela. Soon after, apartheid ended. When all people were allowed to vote in 1994, the African National Congress gained control of the Parliament and Mandela became President. I 1996, a new democratic constitution was ac opted for the Republic of South Africa.

Question: What African names were assoc ated with independence movements?

Answer:

1. Kwame Nkrumah - The British Gol Coast became an independent Ghana in 195 under his leadership.

2. *Jomo Kenyatta* - He was the first pres dent of Kenya after it received independenc from Britain in 1963.

3. Mobutu Sese Seko - He became leader (Zaire after receiving independence from Be gium in 1960. He ruled through military forc Seko took wealth for himself and attempted eliminate colonial and communist influenc from the country.

Definition: Rwandan Genocide, 1994

Two rival ethnic groups exist in Rwanda. Hutus (the majority) and Tutsis. For centurie there has been conflict. In 1994, violence w: triggered after Rwandan President Juvén Habyarimana, a Hutu, died in a plane cras Hutus accused the Tutsis of shooting dow the plane. In reaction, genocide occurred. F about 100 days an estimated 800,000 Tuts were killed, mostly by Hutus. Many Tutsis fl the country until the Rwandan Patriotic Fro (RPF) restored order.

Definition: War in Darfur

Darfur is a region of Sudan that borde neighboring Chad. In 2003, the governme was accused of oppressing non-Arab African The Sudan Liberation Army (SLA) and Justi and Equality Movement (JEM) took to arr in protest. The Sudanese government foug back, thus creating a civil war. A group loyal the government, the Janjaweed, forcefully r

oved non-Arab Africans to the border, killing
any in the process.

Over the next decade, 3-5 million Sudanese
ople were brought to camps patrolled by the
njaweed. Statistics on the killings are diffi-
lt to obtain, but the UN estimated that over
0,000 people died from starvation or killing
the first five years of relocation.

THE MODERN WORLD

efinition: Developing/Developed Nations

Developing nations are those who are slow-
becoming industrialized. Developed nations
ve established themselves as having manu-
cturing centers and more advanced econo-
ies. The fastest industrializing nations since
00 have been Asian countries like China and
dia, and Latin American ones such as Brazil.
The term *Third World* is usually associated
ith poorer, or developing nations. The term
as used during the Cold War to identify coun-
es not aligned with either the United States
the Soviet Union.

efinition: Green Revolution, c1950-1970

New farming techniques, chemical pesti-
des, and fertilizers increased crop yields in
e twentieth century. More food for consump-
on meant less world hunger. Think: Lettuce is
een, and so was this revolution.

efinition: European Union, 1992

The Maastricht Treaty of 1992 established
e European Union a year later. The EU is a
olitical union between certain European Na-
ons. The EU allows people to travel freely
rough member nations, creates common leg-
lation, and operates on the currency of the
uro. In 2009, Greece and other nations be-
an to have severe economic problems which
reatened the stability of the EU. This led to a
ries of bailouts from economically stronger
members, specifically Germany.

Definition: Global Interdependence

In recent years, nations have become dependent on each other. They also can have
their livelihood affected by events thousands
of miles away. In 2008, when the stock market took a dive in the United States, markets
around the world were affected. When the 2004
tsunami hit Indonesia, or the 2010 earthquake
devastated Haiti, the rest of the world helped
out. With information readily available on tele-
vision and the internet, the entire world has become a network of dependent nations.

The world has come together to condemn
terrorism as well. After al Qaeda attacked the
United States on September 11, 2001, other nations helped the United States fight the *War on
Terror* by supplying intelligence and land for
military bases.

Definition: G-8, G-20

A great example of global interdependence
is the Group of Eight. The G-8 consists of
some of the strongest industrial nations in the
world, including the United States, Germany,
Britain, and Japan. Every year they hold a summit meeting to discuss the state of the world,
and ways to solve global problems.

There's also a Group of Twenty (G-20) which
is a summit composed of finance leaders from
twenty major economic world powers. They meet
to discuss the stability of the world's economy.

Question: What are some of the environ-
mental problems plaguing the Earth today?

Answer:

1. Deforestation - Destruction of trees, notably near the Amazon River in South America.

2. Desertification - The expanding of deserts,
as seen in the Sahel of the Sahara.

3. Climate Change - There has been an in-

crease in average world temperatures. Many scientists believe this is influenced by pollution. Others believe climate change is natural. Nonetheless, increases in temperature can affect crop yields, water depletion, and could increase the strength of violent storms.

4. Ozone Depletion - The ozone layer protects people from the sun's ultraviolet rays. Chemicals released into the atmosphere could deplete this barrier. In 1962, American Rachel Carson wrote a book called *Silent Spri* in which she helped spark an environmen movement to ban certain chemical pestici that could harm the environment.

5. Nuclear *Proliferation* - This means spread of nuclear weapons around the wor Neighboring nations with unfriendly relatio such as India and Pakistan, have nuclear wea ons that could do serious harm to the envir ment if deployed.

Gamal Abdel Nasser's actions in 1956
used controversy along the
A) Indian Ocean
B) Suez Canal
C) Dead Sea
D) Atlantic Ocean

A goal of the 1979 Iranian Revolution was to
A) establish a state based on capitalism and
economic growth
B) remove Western influences from the
country
C) create a secular society
D) give more rights to Iranian women

The Camp David Accords brought peace
ostly between Israel and
A) Egypt
B) the PLO
C) Iran
D) Syria

OPEC influences the world in the twenty-
st century because they
A) have great control over oil prices
B) encourage revolution in the Middle East
C) provide new ways to control global warm-
ing
D) make sure trees are replanted after defor-
estation

5. Which was true of apartheid in South Africa
in the twentieth century?
A) It always had the support of Great Britain
and the United States
B) Minority whites limited rights of the majority African population
C) Hindus and Muslims lived in a state of
segregation
D) The African National Congress and Afrikaners historically supported one another

6. Kwame Nkrumah and Jomo Kenyatta were
associated with
A) establishing a constitution in South Africa
B) bringing peace to Darfur
C) resistance to apartheid
D) African independence movements

7. Regarding Rwanda in 1994, most of the peo-
ple killed were
A) Sudanese
B) South African
C) Tutsi
D) Hutu

8. Which of the following South American
countries has seen the most amount of indus-
trial growth in the twenty-first century?
A) Peru
B) Ecuador
C) Brazil
D) Bolivia

9. Which of the following is an example of global interdependence?

A) A stock market crash in the United States affecting the economy in Japan

B) Massive industrialization in India creating a booming economy

C) Forests being destroyed near the Amazon River disturbing the local ecosystem

D) Middle Eastern protests for democracy leading to the overthrow of a dictator

10. The Green Revolution was most associate with

A) limiting the amount of crude oil extracte from Middle Eastern countries

B) the elimination of pesticides and chem cals from certain household products

C) reducing the affects of man-made glob warming

D) increasing the amount of food suitable fo consumption around the planet

B. Egypt took control of the Suez Canal, reby creating the Suez Crisis. After internal forces took it back, the United Nations ssured for its return to Egypt.

B. In the Iranian Revolution, the pro-West ah was taken out of power. Ayatollah Khoini and his followers looked to establish a te based on Islamic law.

A. In the agreement, Israel was recognized as ation and the Sinai Peninsula was returned Egypt.

A. OPEC is the Organization of Petroleum porting Countries. They control the supply much of the world's oil.

B. Apartheid segregated and limited the hts of black Africans. Apartheid was admin-rated by South Africa's minority white popu-ion.

6. **D**. Both leaders helped bring about independence…Kenyatta for Kenya, and Nkrumah for Ghana.

7. **C**. The Hutus targeted the Tutsis with violence. The tribes had been adversaries for centuries.

8. **C**. Brazil has been industrializing at an enormous speed. Rio de Janeiro was chosen to host the 2016 Summer Olympic Games.

9. **A**. Global interdependence occurs when countries thousands of miles away become dependent upon one another. The global economy is an example of such interdependence, as the stock markets around the world affect each other.

10. **D**. The Green Revolution increased the amount of food available for world consumption. Try to remember that lettuce is green, as was this revolution.

Writing a DBQ

Some state tests, and the AP World History Exam, use a ***Document Based Question*** (DBQ) essay format. In this task, the test will give you a series of about ten documents. It is your job to group these documents into different categories, and argue a thesis.

By now, your teacher should have showed you a long rubric illustrating how the DBQ is scored. We are here to trim the fat out of that long rubric. You will do great on the DBQ if you answer yes to the following:

1. Did I put the documents into proper groups?
2. Did I include the right information from the documents?
3. Do I have a detailed thesis?
4. Is my outside information impressive?
5. Did I prove my thesis?

If you are writing for an AP class:
6. Did I use all of the documents?
7. Did I write with *exhaustive breadth*?

Let's assume we have a DBQ that offers the following question:

1. What were the social, economic, and political causes for world conflicts after 1800 CE?

No Bull Tip #1, Grouping Documents
Every DBQ sets up a task that will divide documents into different groups. Read the question first, and then make a grid that looks like this:

Document Letter

Social	
Economic	
Political	

As you go through each document, put its letter in the proper place on the grid. Let's assume that your documents are as follows:

A. Primary source from a Chinese Boxer Rebel expressing anger for the spread of Christianity in China.

B. Newspaper article detailing the assassination of Archduke Franz Ferdinand.

C. Speech from United States President Dwight Eisenhower detailing the Domino Theory.

D. Map of the world showing the transfer of opium throughout the British Empire.

E. A Sudanese man's appeal to the United Nations for support and aid to the people of Darfur.

F. Map showing the raw materials available to Japan after their invasion of Manchuria in 1931.

G. NATO statement expressing concern for the people of Bosnia who were the targets of ethnic cleansing.

H. Eighteenth century newspaper article explaining opportunities in the mining of diamonds in South Africa.

I. Nationalistic speech from Otto von Bismarck expressing the desire to accumulate territory.

After flipping through the documents, you have determined that your grid now looks like this:

Document Letter

Social	**A, E, G**
Economic	**D, F, H**
Political	**B, C, I**

Note: *On state tests, they will tell you how many documents you need to use. On AP Tests, it is recommended that you use ALL OF THE DOCUMENTS.* When citing documents, you can either say: "In Document I, Bismarck says..." or you can just put (Doc. I) at the end of the sentence. Now the essay will come in well-organized paragraphs.

o Bull Tip #2, What to Include From the Documents

You should keep the following in mind when you are reading over the documents:
1. What is this about?
2. Where does it fit in my essay?
3. Who is writing this, and what is their bias or point of view?
4. What outside information can I use for this? (explained below)

o Bull Tip #3, You Better Have a Strong Thesis

A DBQ wants you to make a thesis. Be warned! Do not just use the sentence they give you in the directions as the thesis. We know that there were economic, political, and social causes of these wars. If you get a little creative, it will help your grade.

Average Thesis: Throughout world history, conflict and war were the result of a multitude of social, economic, and political factors.

Better Thesis: Economic factors were the most important causes for conflict after 1840, as the need for resources led to further social and political unrest.

The second thesis shows a greater level of creative and critical thinking. If you can go the extra mile, then do so. If not, that's OK, just try to make it up with your outside information.

Tip #4, Exhaustive Outside Information

No Bull, you need to have a lot of outside information. As you go through each document, down notes in the margins. Your documents should be drowning in ink by the time you are do Give anything...ANYTHING...relevant that is not in the documents. For example, Documen deals with the Opium War. In the margin write down *"Treaty of Nanjing," "Hong Kong goes Britain."* Any note about the Taping Rebellion, or spheres of influence would also be a great dition of outside information.

I don't see anything about Hitler's invasion of Poland in the documents. That's political outs information.

I don't see anything about Rwandan Genocide. That's social outside information.

I don't see anything about the Suez Crisis. That's economic outside information.

Throw it all in. You need *exhaustive breadth,* or a great scope of knowledge, to get the high grade. It's all about what you put into your sentences. Some state tests request that you cite yo outside knowledge. Cite your "knowledge" or "outside information" as (K) or (O.I.).

Normal Breadth: Archduke Franz Ferdinand's assassination was the spark that led to Wo War I.

Exhaustive Breadth: On June 28, 1914, Austrian Archduke Franz Ferdinand was assassina in Sarajevo by a Serbian nationalist named Gavrilo Princip. The assassination set off a chain rea tion that caused World War I.

Normal Breadth: The presence of diamonds in modern-day South Africa led to the fighting the Boer Wars between the British and the Dutch.

Exhaustive Breadth: After European nations divided up Africa at the Berlin Conference, the was still conflict in South Africa, as the superior British military defeated the Dutch in the Bo Wars c1900.

Do you see the difference? Throw in a fact here, a year there. That's exhaustive breadth!

0 More Practice Questions

The Neolithic Revolution was important because it
A) established new writing systems in Mesopotamia
B) paved the way for independent nation states
C) provided agricultural techniques necessary for permanent settlements
D) led people to question natural rights for the first time

Civilizations tend to develop near
A) rivers
B) mountain ranges
C) equatorial latitudes
D) the center of land masses

Christianity and Judaism have similarities in their
A) high holy day observances
B) beliefs in monotheism
C) acceptance of reincarnation
D) teachings that all living creatures have souls

All of the following were associated with riting systems EXCEPT:
A) ziggurats
B) glyphs
C) cuneiform
D) hieroglyphics

- Gupta Empire
- Deccan Plateau
- Ganges River

All of the above are associated with which modern-day country?
A) India
B) Mongolia
C) Bangladesh
D) Afghanistan

6. *"If a man destroys the eye of another man, they shall destroy his eye."*
The above quote could be found in
A) Justinian's Code
B) Hammurabi's Code
C) Twelve Tables of Law
D) Pericles' Direct Democracy Decree

Use the following Speakers to help you answer 7-9:

Speaker 1: The teachings of Islam should be followed in every aspect of life.
Speaker 2: Everything in life is suffering. One must break free from materialism and desire to find enlightenment.
Speaker 3: Good deeds are needed to elevate one's status in the next life. Bad deeds would make one receive a lower status.
Speaker 4: One must be aware of the proper relationships within family and society.

7. Who of the above would be a member of the Hindu faith?
A) Speaker 1
B) Speaker 2
C) Speaker 3
D) Speaker 4

8. Who of the above believes in Sharia law?
A) Speaker 1
B) Speaker 2
C) Speaker 3
D) Speaker 4

9. Speaker 4 most likely adheres to
A) Shintoism
B) Confucianism
C) Daoism
D) Animism

10. The Tang and the Song were associated with the development of all of the following EXCEPT:

A) paper currency

B) porcelain

C) movable type printing

D) caravel ships

11. Chivalry of the knight in feudal European culture was similar to what Japanese code?

A) Kabuki

B) Haiku

C) Bushido

D) Shintoism

12. Direct democracy in Greece during the Age of Pericles involved

A) electing representatives to a life-term in the Senate

B) allowing citizens to create laws as an assembly

C) the election of both men and women to judicial offices

D) two kings ruling on behalf of the people

13.

The above architecture is considered

A) Classical

B) Baroque

C) Gothic

D) Romanesque

14. Which agricultural technique was us first?

A) Slash-and-burn farming

B) Three Field System

C) Use of the Seed Drill

D) Wheelbarrow farming

15. The Silk Roads linked all of the followi cultures EXCEPT:

A) Rome

B) China

C) India

D) Mesoamerica

16. Hellenistic Culture can best be described

A) an Egyptian religious movement

B) a combination of cultures within Alexa der the Great's Empire

C) the breaking away of the Byzantine E pire from Rome

D) the abandonment of Confucianism in t Qin Dynasty

17. Legalism of the Chinese was similar to t writings of Niccolò Machiavelli in that both

A) celebrated freedom of speech as a gua anteed right

B) emphasized the importance of priva property

C) celebrated the concept of a limited mo archy

D) believed that citizens had to be ruled I strict and powerful governments

e the following map for Questions 18 and

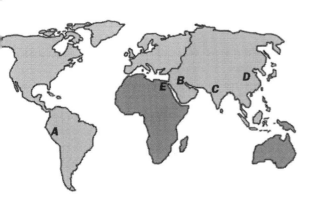

. In which of the above would one find the
cient civilizations of Harappa and Mohenjo-
ro?

A) A
B) B
C) C
D) D
E) E

. Which area would be in the Andes Moun-
n Range?

A) A
B) B
C) C
D) D
E) E

. Who was at the bottom of the social pyra-
id of European feudalism?

A) Lords
B) Vassals
C) Knights
D) Serfs

. The development of the Russian language
as most dependent on which alphabet?

A) Cyrillic
B) Greek
C) Latin
D) Arabic

22. The schism of the Church that occurred in
1054 led to

A) new Protestant sects in Eastern Europe
B) Roman Catholicism in the West and East-
ern Orthodox in the Byzantine Empire
C) England becoming Anglican
D) a Pope in Rome, and a Pope in France

23. The Crusades were fought over

A) a controversy involving the selling of
sacraments
B) control of the Holy Land
C) land disputes within the feudal system
D) a split in the Catholic Church

24. Thomas Aquinas and Averroës were similar
in that both

A) were scholars of Islam
B) used Greek philosophy in their study of
religion
C) were excommunicated for their beliefs
D) expressed a devotion to polytheism

25. A direct result of the Crusades was

A) a split in the Catholic Church
B) European control of Jerusalem
C) an increase in cultural diffusion
D) the fall of the Ottoman Empire

26. What impact did the bubonic plague have
on the Catholic Church in the fourteenth century?

A) There was a decreased faith in the Church
as prayers went unanswered
B) Because of the need for prayer, the
Church's power grew by the end of the
plague
C) Many Catholics converted to Judaism and
Islam
D) The plague directly caused the Protestant
Reformation

27. Terrace farming was used extensively by which Empire of the Andes Mountains?

A) Mayan
B) Toltec
C) Aztec
D) Incan

28. Today, there is an incomplete history of the Mayan Empire because the

A) wars between the Aztecs and Mayans wiped out most written records
B) Mayans did not have a written form of record-keeping
C) Spanish burned or destroyed much of the historical record
D) language can't be interpreted

29. Pyramids in Egypt and structures like the one above from Native America both

A) were made out of clay
B) look similar despite a lack of cultural contact
C) had no mortar to hold the stones in place
D) were used for human sacrifice

30. Besides the Indus, which river was most associated with early civilizations in India?

A) Nile
B) Yangtze
C) Tigris
D) Ganges

31. Bantu migrations were most important Africa because they

A) led to the development of languages used today
B) opened Africa to trade with European tions
C) eliminated reliance on hunting and ga ering
D) blended both Arabic and African cultu

32. Marco Polo's travels were most similar those of

A) Suleiman the Magnificent
B) Mansa Musa
C) Shah Abbas
D) Ibn Battuta

33. All of the following empires were asso ated with the subcontinent of India EXCEP

A) Mughal Empire
B) Gupta Empire
C) Mauryan Empire
D) Umayyad Empire

34. Mansa Musa

A) helped spread Islam to the African Kir dom of Mali
B) was a great traveler who went from A rica to Asia
C) was the first African king to sell his pe ple into slavery
D) ended the gold-salt trade and isola western Africa

. Which of the following reflects the reli-
ous teachings of John Calvin?
A) Divine right was not protected by the Bi-
ble
B) The use of icons was necessary for suc-
cessful prayer
C) A person's salvation was predetermined
by God
D) The Pope was the highest authority in
Christianity

. Pope Alexander VI hoped to bring peace
tween Spain and Portugal in 1493 by
A) instituting a line of demarcation for ex-
ploration
B) taking land from both nations and adding
it to the Church
C) outlawing all further conquests in the
New World
D) making Catholic nations share gold taken
from their colonies

'. Shortly before 1500, Portugal took advan-
ge of the East Coast of Africa because of its
A) abundance of slave labor
B) riches of gold, ivory, animal skins, and
other resources
C) market for selling finished textile goods
D) strategic location to other markets in the
Indian Ocean

3. The Peace of Augsburg and the Thirty
ears' War both reflected the
A) severity of religious division in Europe
B) need for the Pope to intervene during the
Age of Exploration
C) popularity of Enlightenment philosophy
D) splits within the Anglican Church of Eng-
land

39. 1. Black Plague
     2. Fall of Rome
     3. Protestant Reformation
     4. Elizabethan Age

Put the above in their proper chronological or-
der.
A) 1 - 2 - 3 - 4
B) 2 - 1 - 4 - 3
C) 1 - 3 - 2 - 4
D) 2 - 1 - 3 - 4

40. Classical ideas regarding humanism and
Western Heritage came from
A) Greece and Rome
B) Byzantium and Constantinople
C) England and France
D) Ancient Mesopotamia

41. Algebra, astronomy, calligraphy and the
Abbasid Empire were all associated with which
region?
A) Asia
B) Middle East
C) Europe
D) Native America

42. The Khmer Empire in the year 1200 was
similar to the ancient Phoenicians in that both
A) established dominance through sea travel
B) produced alphabets that were adopted by
the west
C) traded extensively in the Mediterranean
D) constructed magnificent Hindu temples

43. Though hundreds of years apart, the Han and Tang dynasties of China both fell partly because of
    A) economic instability and famine
    B) religious persecution of the people
    C) overexpansion of both Empires into parts of India
    D) discontent over a lack of civil liberties

44. Traditional African and Native American cultures c1000 CE were based on
    A) laissez-faire capitalism
    B) industrialization
    C) a command economy
    D) agriculture

45. Which of the following Empires controlled the most territory at the peak of their rule?
    A) Mongol Empire
    B) Byzantine Empire
    C) Alexander the Great
    D) Holy Roman Empire

46. Of the following explorers, the one with the greatest fleet of ships was
    A) Vasco da Gama
    B) Christopher Columbus
    C) Zheng He
    D) Ferdinand Magellan

47. The system of mercantilism involved
    A) developing large standing armies
    B) acquiring raw materials from colonies
    C) gaining military bases around the Pacific Ocean
    D) seeking alliances with nations within Central Europe

48. Louis XIV's absolute rule in France, and Joseph Stalin's totalitarian government in Soviet Union both
    A) commanded all economic production
    B) divided all land among the peasants
    C) preached atheism
    D) limited political civil liberties

49. Which of the following is paired with proper writing?
    A) John Locke - *Two Treatises of Gove ment*
    B) Mao Zedong - *The Social Contract*
    C) Simón Bolívar - *Little Red Book of Q tations*
    D) Maximilien Robespierre - *The Prince*

50. ***"Man is born free, and everywhere he in chains."***
    The intention of this quote by Jean-Jacqu Rousseau was to
    A) defend absolutism and divine right
    B) encourage the disobeying of unjust law
    C) limit the power of the Roman Catho Church in everyday affairs
    D) bring more rights to workers in lat unions

51. In the seventeenth and eighteenth cen ries, Enlightenment thinkers wanted a soci where
    A) the factors of production could be own by the people
    B) natural rights would be protected
    C) the government would take its *hands* the economy
    D) absolute monarchs could rule with divi right

The theocracy of Egypt and the Mandate Heaven of China were similar to European as regarding

A) The Protestant Reformation
B) Divine Right
C) Enlightened Despotism
D) Imperialism

Which style was a reaction to baroque architecture of the early eighteenth century?

A) Neoclassical
B) Impressionism
C) Realism
D) Gothic

Which was true of the punishments of Galileo and Socrates?

A) Socrates admitted his methods were flawed and was released
B) Galileo was put to death for his claims
C) Socrates died for his beliefs while Galileo did not
D) Both men were set free after protests of the people

• Humanism
• *The David*
• The Medici Family

ll of the above were associated with

A) The Dark Ages
B) The Enlightenment
C) The Renaissance
D) The Scientific Revolution

56. Which was a goal of Peter the Great in his westernization of Russia in the early eighteenth century?

A) Ridding the country of Mongol influence
B) Taking part in the Industrial Revolution
C) Securing overseas colonies in Africa
D) Adopting the teachings of Karl Marx

57. Those of Spanish descent that could hold high office in the New World were called

A) Peninsulares
B) Creoles
C) Mestizos
D) Mulattos

58. José San Martin and Simón Bolívar were mostly associated with

A) philosophical writings of the Enlightenment
B) Latin American independence movements
C) the divine right theory of government
D) slave revolts in the Caribbean

59. In the nineteenth century, demands in the Western Hemisphere for self-rule were inspired by

A) European Enlightenment thought
B) promises of economic supremacy
C) a desire for religious freedoms
D) support for absolutism

60. Maximilien Robespierre's Reign of Terror aimed to

A) assassinate Enlightenment thinkers such as John Locke
B) eliminate all opposition to the French Revolution
C) destroy the Committee of Public Safety
D) restore the Bourbon family to the throne

61. All of the following were examples of cultural diffusion EXCEPT:
   A) Columbian Exchange
   B) Silk Roads
   C) Westernization of Russia
   D) Continental System

62. Which of the following was true of the Napoleonic Code?
   A) It reflected mostly all of Justinian's Code
   B) Women's rights were limited, as was freedom of speech
   C) The Code severely limited the ruler's power
   D) It was written to increase Jacobin authority

63. A coup d'état was accomplished by
   A) Simón Bolívar
   B) John Locke
   C) Mao Zedong
   D) Napoleon Bonaparte

64. All of the following were associated with the Industrial Revolution in England in the late eighteenth century EXCEPT:
   A) Steam powered vessels
   B) Urbanization
   C) Entrepreneur opportunities
   D) Socialism

65. The Sepoy Mutiny and the Boxer Rebellion were similar in that both
   A) began in western China
   B) led to the development of industrialization in Asia
   C) failed to put an end to European imperialism
   D) ended the practice of spheres of influence

66. How did the Meiji Era of the nineteenth century affect Japan in the twentieth century
   A) Massive industrialization transformed Japan into an imperial power
   B) A lasting peace led to the development of new religious practices
   C) There was an increase in European sphere of influence within Japan in the twentieth century
   D) Revolutions in Japan led to the removal of the Emperor

67. Which of the following artists was associated with the impressionism and post-impressionism movements of the nineteenth century
   A) Rembrandt van Rijn
   B) Jan van Eyck
   C) Vincent Van Gogh
   D) Jan Vermeer

68. In laissez-faire economics, Adam Smith argued that governments should
   A) provide the greatest good for the greatest amount of people
   B) abandon capitalism in favor of socialism
   C) allow for free markets to trade without government intervention
   D) regulate the stock market to prevent unfair trading practices

69. Which of the following is matched up with the territory they conquered?
   A) Hernando Cortés – Aztec Empire
   B) Adolf Hitler - Soviet Union
   C) Napoleon Bonaparte - Britain
   D) Kublai Khan - Japan

1. Age of Enlightenment
2. French Revolution
3. American Revolution
4. Latin American Independence Movements

t the above in their proper chronological or-
r

A) 1 - 4 - 3 - 2
B) 3 - 1 - 4 - 2
C) 1 - 3 - 2 - 4
D) 2 - 4 - 1 - 3

. Otto von Bismarck's newly unified Germa-
gained land
A) from the Pope
B) through international conflict
C) from the Eastern Orthodox Church
D) after a land purchase from Russia

. A major cause for massive emigration from
land c1845 was
A) war with the British mainland
B) failure of the potato crop
C) Napoleon's invasion
D) religious wars in Northern Ireland

. By 1900, which country gained the most
nd from the Berlin Conference and the Age
`Asian Imperialism?
A) Britain
B) France
C) Netherlands
D) Germany

. Whose scientific theories were used to jus-
fy imperialist activity in the late nineteenth
ntury?
A) Albert Einstein
B) Guglielmo Marconi
C) Sigmund Freud
D) Charles Darwin

75. The Treaty of Versailles provided for
A) an international peace-keeping organiza-
tion
B) aid to Germany to help rebuild defense
plants
C) the restoration of monarchs to Spain and
France
D) an official surrender of the Allied Powers

76. Protests in Amritsar, India and St. Peters-
burg, Russia in the early twentieth century end-
ed when
A) citizens received reforms from the gov-
ernment
B) the military killed many demonstrators
C) new elections were scheduled
D) communist demands were met

77. Which of the following would complete
section A on this outline?
I. World Revolutions
A) Causes of the _____
1. World War I devastation
2. Workers wanting better living conditions
3. Support for the writings of Karl Marx

What should go in A on the outline?
A) Bolshevik Revolution
B) Rise of Joseph Stalin
C) Fall of Communism
D) Rise of Peter the Great

78. Joseph Stalin's Five Year Plan in the Soviet
Union and Mao Zedong's Great Leap Forward
in China were similar in that both
A) attempted to dramatically increase pro-
duction
B) had universal support among the people
C) were considered successful by historians
D) allowed unions to collectively bargain for
wages and reforms

79. All of the following were supporters of the Allied powers in World War II EXCEPT:

A) France
B) Great Britain
C) Japan
D) China

80. Which of the following was used by Joseph Stalin, but NOT Adolf Hitler?

A) A secret police
B) Immense propaganda campaigns
C) Division of land among the people
D) Use of work camps for those considered enemies of the state

81. Which of the following was true of *glasnost* in the late twentieth century?

A) Mao Zedong welcomed criticism from the people
B) There was strict enforcement of communism in the Soviet Union
C) The Cultural Revolution brought Roman Catholicism to China
D) New ideas from the Soviet people were welcomed

82. Dr. Martin Luther King, Jr. and Mohandas Gandhi were similar in that

A) the writings of Machiavelli were influential to their beliefs
B) neither were imprisoned for their acts of protest
C) violence was used to achieve civil rights
D) both disobeyed government laws seen as unjust

83. Mohandas Gandhi's Salt March was most similar to the actions taken by which organization in the twentieth century?

A) African National Congress
B) Tamil Tigers
C) NATO
D) Taliban

84. Which of the following was the result of the others?

A) Weakness of the Weimar Republic
B) Rise of Adolf Hitler
C) Economic discontent
D) Resentment of the Treaty of Versailles

85. All of the following were examples of Anti-Semitism EXCEPT:

A) Kristallnacht
B) Camp David Accords
C) Pogroms
D) Dreyfus Affair

86. How did the partition of India in 1947 compare to the reunification of Germany in 1989?

A) Unlike Germany, India's partition was accompanied by religious conflict
B) Germany unified under communism whereas India did not
C) Both processes were accompanied by w
D) India remained one country, while Germany's reunification was short-lived

87. The policy of détente was used during the Cold War to

A) decrease the level of political tension
B) increase the manufacturing of nuclear weapons
C) help return Cuba to its pre-communist state
D) stop the spread of communism to Korea and Vietnam

Which of the following examples of geno-
e took place in Southeast Asia?
A) Pol Pot's massacre of opponents to the
Khmer Rouge
B) Hitler's Final Solution
C) Hutu killings of the Tutsis
D) Armenian massacres during and after
World War I

I. Human Rights Violations
A) Holocaust in Europe
B) _____
C) Ethnic Cleansing in Bosnia
D) Rwandan genocide

the above outline, what could fit in letter B?
A) War in Darfur
B) Green Revolution
C) Perestroika
D) Treaty of Versailles

. The Tamil Tigers struggled for
A) freedoms of speech and assembly
B) a permanent homeland
C) women's rights
D) elimination of the caste system

. Who of the following gave significant
ghts to women?
A) Muhammad Ali Jinnah
B) Mao Zedong
C) Louis XIV
D) Genghis Khan

. Westernization was an objective of all of
e following EXCEPT:
A) Reza Pahlavi, the Shah of Iran
B) Peter the Great of Russia
C) Emperor Mutsohito of Japan
D) The Taliban of Afghanistan

93. In 1989, the government of Deng Xiaoping
responded to protests in Tiananmen Square by
A) displaying a strong military presence
B) passing the Four Modernizations
C) eliminating the One-Child Policy
D) extending rights to freedom of assembly

94. Mikhail Gorbachev's perestroika was most
similar to which other communist policy?
A) Lenin's NEP
B) Stalin's totalitarian rule
C) Mao's Great Leap Forward
D) The Cultural Revolution of China

95. Which of the following was an example of
Zionism?
A) Balfour Declaration
B) Yom Kippur War
C) Russian pogroms
D) Dreyfus Affair

96. Which statement is true of the twenty-first
century when compared to the fifteenth century?
A) There were many more religious sects in
the fifteenth century than there are today
B) The world in the twenty-first century has
a greater degree of global interdependence
C) There is less pollution today because of
legislation looking to decrease carbon emissions
D) The fifteenth century presented a greater
degree of democratic reforms

97. The Neolithic Revolution and the Green
Revolution were similar in that both
A) were limited to Europe and Asia
B) decreased the need to settle into perma-
nent civilizations
C) increased the life expectancy of certain
populations
D) led to divisions among religious sects

98. Which is considered to be a primary source?

A) A biography of the life of Maria Theresa

B) Napoleon's speech to his troops at Austerlitz

C) Encyclopedia entry on John Locke

D) Textbook chapter on the French Revolution

99. All of the following leaders preached religious tolerance EXCEPT:

A) King Nebuchadnezzar

B) Akbar the Great

C) Asoka

D) Suleiman the Magnificent

100. Which statement comparing the eighteenth century Industrial Revolution to indutrialization in the Modern Era is true?

A) Unlike the first Industrial Revolution, today's industrialization is more of an urbaphenomenon

B) The earlier Industrial Revolution used factory system to produce finished good whereas modern day nations have abadoned using factories for production

C) Only recent industrialization has creatpollution

D) Industrialization in recent years is not dependent on energy resources found near

Answers and Explanations

C. The Neolithic Revolution's new agricultural techniques led to permanent settlements and a decreased dependence on nomadic lifestyle. All over the world civilizations emerged.

A. Civilizations develop near water because of farming and trading opportunities. In Mesopotamia, the rivers are the Tigris and Euphrates. In China, you should know the Huang He (Yellow) and Yangtze. In India, the Ganges and Indus are vital for survival.

B. Both religions believe in one God. This is called monotheism. A belief in multiple gods is called polytheism.

A. Ziggurats were religious structures built in Sumer of ancient Mesopotamia. Glyphs were symbols used by the Mayan Empire. Hieroglyphics were written in Egypt. Cuneiform was from ancient Sumer.

A. India. Try to remember DIG...Deccan, India, Ganges (Gupta).

B. "An eye for an eye" is from Hammurabi's Code. The code applied to everyone, but remember...it punished the poor and gave women a lower status.

C. Speaker 3 is talking about the relationship between karma, reincarnation, and the caste system. According to Hinduism, better deeds will elevate one to a higher caste in the next life.

A. Sharia involves a relationship between Islam and political, economic, and social affairs.

9. **B**. Confucianism is concerned with the five relationships. In addition, filial piety stresses the importance of respecting one's elders.

10. **D**. Caravel ships were designed by the Portuguese as a means for exploration in the fifteenth century.

11. **C**. Like chivalry, the bushido code of Japan stressed a similar importance on bravery. The samurai warrior was expected to honor all obligations.

12. **B**. The Greek direct democracy allowed average male citizens to take part in lawmaking. Women and slaves were denied such participation in government.

13. **A**. The Parthenon is a well-known classical structure. Classical buildings are symmetrical, and many also contain columns. Classical architecture was copied all over the Western World.

14. **A**. Slash-and-burn farming was associated with early human settlements. Trees were burned to create open fields. Then, the ashes from the fire would be used to fertilize the farmland.

15. **D**. Mesoamerica is in the New World, and therefore isolated from the Silk Roads. The New World would be isolated from all foreign cultures until the Age of Exploration.

16. **B**. Alexander the Great amassed an impressive Empire which created Hellenistic Culture. A blending of Egyptian, Persian, Greek, and Indian ideals was accomplished through trade.

17. **D.** Both Legalism and Machiavelli's *The Prince* emphasized the importance of strict rule and order. The belief was that if the ruler gave too many rights to their citizens, the people would strip them of their power.

18. **C.** Harappa and Mohenjo-daro were in the Indus River Valley in modern-day India.

19. **A.** The South American civilizations of the Chavín and Inca were established in the Andes.

20. **D.** Serfs were bound to the land in European feudalism. Czar Alexander II did not emancipate (free) Russian serfs until the middle of the nineteenth century.

21. **A.** The Cyrillic alphabet of Russia has Slavic roots and was influenced by Saint Cyril.

22. **B.** There was too great of a distance between the Byzantine Empire in the East, and the Roman Catholic Church of Rome. There were arguments over religious practices, notably the use of icons. The religion in the East became Eastern Orthodox. Be careful with choice D...that refers to the Great Schism of the Middle Ages where two Popes claimed legitimacy.

23. **B.** Christians and Muslims fought a Holy War after Pope Urban II called for a Crusade in 1095. The objective was to control the Holy Land in and around Jerusalem.

24. **B.** Both philosophers combined the philosophy of Aristotle with theology (study of religious faith). Aquinas wrote the *Summa Theologica*. Averroës wrote *The Incoherence of the Incoherence*.

25. **C.** Although violent, the Crusades led to a increase of trade between Europe and the Midd East.

26. **A.** Although one would expect more peop to attend Church services during the plague, the was an overall decrease in faith because praye went unanswered.

27. **D.** Terrace farming is an agricultural techniqu used to level off the slopes of mountains and hil This was done all over the world and notably the Andes Mountains by the Incan Empire.

28. **C.** The Conquistadors believed that May: religious writings were pagan and dangerou They burned most of the written record.

29. **B.** Although from different ends of the glob both structures have wide bases that narrow t wards the top.

30. **D.** The Ganges River has great significance the people of India.

31. **A.** The Bantu-speaking people migrated : over sub-Saharan Africa (south of the Saha Desert). Today, many African languages ha roots in Bantu. Swahili is also big in Africa, but came much later after Arabic contact.

32. **D.** Ibn Battuta was the great traveler of Afri in the middle of the fourteenth century. He visit many of the thriving cultures of the world.

33. **D.** The Umayyads built one of the early Mu lim Empires that existed west of the subcontine of modern-day India.

34. **A.** King Mansa Musa of Mali went on the h: (pilgrimage to Mecca), and helped spread Isla to his African Kingdom.

5. **C.** Calvinism was a sect of Christianity that merged during the Protestant Reformation. John Calvin preached predestination, or the belief that one's path to salvation had already been determined.

6. **A.** The Pope's Line of Demarcation divided land in the New World between the Spanish and Portuguese. Spain received the land to the west of the line. Portugal received what was east (in modern-day Brazil). The Treaty of Tordesillas of 1794 moved the line a bit to the west to give Portugal more territory.

7. **B.** Eastern Africa offered many valuable resources to the Portuguese before 1500. Slave trading was more abundant later.

8. **A.** The 1555 Peace of Augsburg allowed princes of Germany to determine if their regions would be Catholic or Protestant. The Thirty Years' War began as a religious conflict in 1618.

9. **D.** Fall of Rome, 476 CE; Black Plague, 1350; Protestant Reformation, c1517; Elizabethan Age, c1580.

10. **A.** Greco-Roman culture influenced humanism and the development of Renaissance culture.

11. **B.** Although some other cultures had calligraphy and astronomical advances, algebra and the Abbasids were relevant to the Middle East.

12. **A.** The Khmer Empire of Southeast Asia established maritime trade connections with China and India. The ancient Phoenicians were sea travelers as well, spreading their culture around the Mediterranean.

43. **A.** The Han and the Tang imposed high taxes and their people suffered from famine. As per the Dynastic Cycle, both dynasties fell.

44. **D.** Both Africa and Native America were predominantly agricultural societies.

45. **A.** Genghis and Kublai Khan proved to be strong leaders, and amassed an Empire that stretched from Asia to Eastern Europe. It even extended into parts of the Middle East. However within a century of Kublai's death, the Mongol Empire lost its strength.

46. **C.** Zheng He explored the Eastern World on behalf of the Ming Dynasty of China. The size of his fleet of ships far exceeded what the Europeans would send out a century later.

47. **B.** Mercantilism involved European countries acting as a Mother Country and extracting resources from their colonies. They sold finished goods to the colonies as well.

48. **D.** Both had absolute, or total control of the country. Many civil liberties were limited, including free speech and fair trials.

49. **A.** Locke's *Two Treatises of Government* was a strong contribution to the Enlightenment. He believed in natural rights such as life, liberty, and property.

50. **B.** Jean-Jacques Rousseau wrote the *Social Contract*. He believed that freedom was important, and people should not obey unjust laws.

51. **B.** Enlightenment thinkers wanted monarchies to limit their power to ensure the protection of natural rights.

52. **B.** Divine Right meant that the absolute ruler was a representative of God. In both Egypt (theocracy) and China (Mandate of Heaven), there was a similar relationship between the ruler and deities.

53. **A.** Neoclassical styles were less ornate than the impressive baroque architecture used in castles like Versailles.

54. **C.** Unlike Socrates who died for his beliefs, Galileo "admitted" his research was flawed. He spent the rest of his life under house-arrest.

55. **C.** All of the terms were from the Renaissance period. Humanism was the spirit of human achievement, and the *David* was sculpted by Michelangelo. The Medici Family of Florence helped sponsor impressive artistic endeavors.

56. **A.** Peter the Great wanted to imitate Western European nations. To become modern, or Western, Russia needed to remove Mongol influences upon their culture. If you said choice B, you are a little early. The Industrial Revolution came decades later.

57. **A.** Peninsulares were atop the pyramid of social power in the New World. They were born in Spain, and then ventured over for political and economic gain.

58. **B.** José San Martin and Simón Bolívar were influential leaders of nineteenth century Latin American independence movements against Spain.

59. **A.** Revolutions in Latin America were inspired by Enlightenment thought and the French Revolution. Countries such as Venezuela, Chile, Brazil, Mexico, and Haiti all fought for independence in the nineteenth century.

60. **B.** Robespierre was a Jacobin whose Committee of Public Safety looked to rid France traitors to the Revolution, such as supporters the King.

61. **D.** Napoleon's Continental System wa blockade that looked to isolate Britain from trading neighbors in Europe. It was unsuccess

62. **B.** The Napoleonic Code was a body of written after the French Revolution. The c limited certain rights of women, as well as fr dom of speech.

63. **D.** Napoleon suddenly seized power wit bloodless overthrow of the government. This tion is known as a coup d'état.

64. **D.** Although socialist ideas were a respo to the Industrial Revolution, socialism never t hold in England.

65. **C.** Both of these violent insurrections w unsuccessful at removing imperialists from In (Sepoy Mutiny) and China (Boxer Rebellion).

66. **A.** After the Meiji Restoration, Japan massi ly industrialized and modernized. In the twenti century, they became a major power that fou wars and imperialized other countries.

67. **C.** Vincent Van Gogh was an impression post-impressionist painter who captured the en tion of a moment.

68. **C.** Laissez-faire means that the governm should take its hands off the economy and all for natural forces to take over.

A. Hernando Cortés conquered the Aztecs. ...ler, Napoleon, and Kublai Khan were all un...cessful in taking over the places they were ...red up with.

C. Age of Enlightenment, c1700-1740; ...erican Revolution, c1776; French Revo-...on, c1789; Latin American Independence ...vements, c1810.

B. Germany unified through "blood and iron." ...a short Seven Weeks' War they took land from ...stria. In the Franco-Prussian War of 1870-71, ...y received the territories of Alsace and Lor-...ne from France.

B. The potato famine in Ireland led to the ...th of an estimated one million people. Many ...migrated to places around the world, notably ...United States.

A. Great Britain acquired a great number of ...lonies, specifically in Africa, India, and China.

D. Darwin's Theory of Evolution led to be-...fs in Social Darwinism, or survival of the fit-...t. Social Darwinism was used to rationalize the ...mination of weaker societies during the Age of ...perialism.

A. The Treaty of Versailles punished Germa-...greatly. It also created an international peace-...eping organization called the League of Na-...ns. Because the League could not raise troops ...fight in international conflicts, Germany was ...le to ignore the provisions of the treaty, and ...militarize.

B. In 1919, the British fired on demonstrators ...the Amritsar Massacre. The Czar did the same ...1905 in St. Petersburg on Bloody Sunday.

77. **A.** The Bolshevik Revolution was caused mostly by high World War I casualties, unhappy workers, and support for a socialist uprising.

78. **A.** Both were attempts at modernization. Stalin set quotas so high, that he never achieved his goals. Mao's Great Leap Forward is considered by historians to be a failure.

79. **C.** Alongside Germany and Italy, Japan was part of the Axis Powers.

80. **C.** Hitler was against communism. Dividing land amongst the people was a communist reform.

81. **D.** Glasnost means openness. The Soviet Union was not historically associated with openness, but under Mikhail Gorbachev there were reforms to change that.

82. **D.** Civil disobedience means to disobey unjust laws. Gandhi and King were also advocates of passive resistance, or nonviolent protests.

83. **A.** The African National Congress used boycotts to try to bring about an end to apartheid in South Africa.

84. **B.** Germany turned to fascism for a number of reasons including economic discontent, hatred of the Treaty of Versailles, and the instability of the Weimar Republic.

85. **B.** The Camp David Accords brought some stability to the Middle East. Egypt recognized Israel as a nation, and Israel returned the Sinai Peninsula.

86. **A.** India's predominantly Hindu population feuded with Muslims in Pakistan. Violence has occurred since partition, especially in the disputed region of Kashmir.

87. **A.** Détente means a lessoning of Cold War tensions between the United States and the Soviet Union. This occurred in the 1970s after a very tense 1960s that included the potentially catastrophic Cuban Missile Crisis.

88. **A.** The Khmer Rouge killed an estimated 2 million Cambodians who were seen as threats to their power. The genocide was led by Pol Pot.

89. **A.** The War in Darfur has led to killings and the relocation of millions in the Sudan.

90. **B.** The Tamil Tigers used military and terror tactics. They failed to establish a separate state in Sri Lanka.

91. **B.** Surprisingly, Communist leaders like Mao Zedong and Joseph Stalin granted more rights to women. However, this generally meant that women would work longer hours, yet still be expected to care for the family.

92. **D.** The Taliban in Afghanistan is fundamentalist (relying on religion) and opposed to westernization.

93. **A.** The Tiananmen Square Massacre was a government response to a protest for democracy in Beijing. Xiaoping's military violently ended the protest. Estimates of the dead and wounded exceeded 2,000.

94. **A.** Both perestroika and Lenin's New E
nomic Policy created capitalist opportunitie
the communist Soviet Union.

95. **A.** The Balfour Declaration came fror
British official who spoke in favor of creatir
Jewish State. Zionism is the support for suc
creation.

96. **B.** Global Interdependence in the twenty-
century is at an all-time high, as developed
developing countries around the world af
the global economy. In addition, the internet
made communication between nations incred
easy. This has created a sense of oneness.

97. **C.** Both revolutions were associated v
increasing the amount of food available for c
sumption. Both increased life expectancy.

98. **B.** A primary source is a first-hand acco
A speech, autobiography, and document fror
historical time period would all be classified to
primary sources.

99. **A.** King Nebuchadnezzar put Jews into c
tivity in ancient times. The other leaders display
acts of religious tolerance during their reigns.

100. **D.** In the first Industrial Revolution t
took place in England, the factors of prod
tion and energy resources were found near
Today, oil from the Middle East is exported
all over the world.

NO BULL
~~NOBLE~~ REVIEW
SHEET

Here are my Review Sheets. Use them often to help you study.

You will notice numbers in brackets after a word or sentence. These are the pages where you can find more detailed information.

Good luck!

Your friend,

Nobley

Most Important Terms of the Course (Numbers in brackets are reference pages in

1. Neolithic Revolution [12]
2. Nomads, and Hunters & Gatherers [12]
3. Ziggurat [13]
4. Cultural Diffusion [12-13]
5. Cuneiform [13]
6. Theocracy [14]
7. Hieroglyphics [14-15]
8. Mandate of Heaven/Dynastic Cycle [19]
9. Tokugawa Shogunate [22]
10. Haiku and Kabuki [22]
11. Harappa and Mohenjo-Daro [23]
12. Caliph [23]
13. Twelve Tables of Law [31]
14. Pax Romana [32]
15. Feudalism [37]
16. Chivalry [38]
17. Three Field System [38]
18. Spanish Inquisition [39]
19. Great Schism [39-40]
20. Bubonic Plague [40]
21. Humanism [40]
22. Printing Press [41]
23. 95 Theses [42]
24. Predestination [43]
25. Bantu-speaking People [47]
26. Ibn Battuta [48]
27. Terrace Farming [49-50]
28. Conquistadors [51]
29. *Encomienda* [51]
30. Middle Passage [51]
31. Mercantilism and Commercial Revolution [51-52]
32. Absolutism [55]
33. Spanish Armada [56]
34. Limited Monarchy [57]
35. Scientific Method [57]
36. Heliocentric Model [57]
37. Enlightenment [57-58]

38. Baroque [59]
39. Enlightened Despots [59]
40. Bourgeoisie [64]
41. Tennis Court Oath [64]
42. Declaration of the Rights of Man [65]
43. Political Spectrum [65]
44. Jacobins [65]
45. Coup d'état [65-66]
46. Napoleonic Code [66]
47. Congress of Vienna [66-67]
48. Urbanization [70-71]
49. Agricultural Revolution [71]
50. Capitalism [71]
51. Socialism [71-72]
52. Potato Famine [72]
53. Berlin Conference [77]
54. Spheres of Influence [78-79]
55. Open Door Policy [79]
56. Meiji Era [79-80]
57. *Lusitania* and Zimmerman Telegram [80-81]
58. League of Nations [81]
59. Treaty of Versailles [81-82]
60. Pogroms [86]
61. Russia's Bloody Sunday [86]
62. NEP [87]
63. USSR [87]
64. Totalitarianism [87]
65. Command Economy/Five-Year Plan [88]
66. Fascism [92]
67. Weimar Republic [92]
68. *Mein Kampf* [93]
69. Appeasement [94]
70. Axis Powers [94]
71. Blitzkrieg [94]
72. Yalta Conference [95]
73. Atomic Bomb [96]
74. United Nations [96]

5. Ghettos [97]
6. Final Solution (Genocide) [97-98]
7. Nuremberg Trials [98]
8. Containment [102, 104]
9. Truman Doctrine and Marshall Plan [102]
0. Berlin Airlift [102-103]
1. NATO and Warsaw Pact [103]
2. Sputnik [103]
3. Berlin Wall [103]
4. Bay of Pigs Invasion [103]
5. Cuban Missile Crisis 103-104]
6. Détente [104]
7. Glasnost and Perestroika [105]
8. Domino Theory [106]
9. Dien Bien Phu [106]
0. Vietcong [107]
1. Khmer Rouge [107]
2. Long March [113]
3. Great Leap Forward [113-114]
4. Cultural Revolution [114]
5. Four Modernizations [114]
6. Tiananmen Square Massacre [114]

Know these terms and you will find success.

97. Three Gorges Dam [115]
98. One-Child Policy [115]
99. Amritsar Massacre [115]
100. Salt March [115]
101. Zionism [120]
102. Balfour Declaration [120]
103. Camp David Accords [120-121]
104. OPEC [121]
105. Taliban [121]
106. Apartheid [122]
107. Developing Nations [123]
108. Green Revolution [123]
109. European Union [123]
110. Global Interdependence [123]

Key Questions

1. What do I need to know about the history at the beginning of my textbook? [12]

2. How did the Han Dynasty govern such a large area? [20]

3. What were the contributions of the early Muslim world? [24-25]

4. What were the differences between Athens and Sparta? [29]

5. What were the contributions of the ancient Greeks? [29-30]

6. How did the Roman Republic function? [31]

7. What were the contributions of Rome? [32]

8. What led to the Fall of Rome? [32]

9. What happened in the schism of 1054? [33]

10. What were the important aspects of the Church during the Middle Ages? [38]

11. What were the causes, events, and results of the Crusades? [38-39]

12. What should I know about Renaissance art and literature? [40-41]

13. What were the causes and results of the Protestant Reformation? [42-43]

14. What motivated Europeans in the Age of Exploration? [50]

15. What was the social hierarchy of the New World under Spanish rule? [52]

16. How did the Enlightenment affect the arts? [58-59]

17. What were the three Estates of France's Old Regime? [63-64]

18. What were Napoleon's three mistakes that led to his downfall? [66]

19. Why has nationalism been a major force in World History? [70]

20. Why did the Industrial Revolution begin in England? [71]

21. What were the textile inventions of the Industrial Revolution? [71]

22. Why did countries want to imperialize? [77]

23. What were the causes and technological innovations of World War I? [80, 81]

24. What were the foreign policy results of World War II? [96]

25. What were the major examples of containment during the Cold War? [104]

26. How did Communism ultimately fall in the Soviet Union? How about in other European tions? [105-106]

27. What happened to India during the Partition? [115-116]

28. What wars were fought between Israel and other Middle East nations from 1956-1973? [12

29. What led to the end of apartheid? [122]

30. What are some of the environmental problems plaguing the Earth today? [123-124]

:ople to Know

1. King Hammurabi [13]
2. Hatshepsut [15]
3. Shi Huangdi [19]
4. Genghis and Kublai Khan [21-22]
5. Zheng He [21]
6. Akbar the Great [23]
7. Socrates, Plato, and Aristotle [30]
8. Julius Caesar [31]
9. Justinian [32-33]
10. Thomas Aquinas [39]
11. Leonardo da Vinci [41]
12. Niccolò Machiavelli [41]
13. Queen Elizabeth I [41]
14. Mansa Musa [48]
15. Louis XIV [55]
16. Maria Theresa [56]
17. Ivan the Terrible [56]
18. Peter the Great [56]
19. Galileo [57]
20. Enlightenment Thinkers (Hobbes, Rousseau, Locke, Voltaire, Montesquieu) [58]
21. Napoleon Bonaparte [65-66]
22. Simón Bolívar [67]
23. Toussaint L'Ouverture [67]
24. Benito Juarez [67]
25. Adam Smith [71]
26. Karl Marx [71-72]

27. Jeremy Bentham and John Stuart Mill [72]
28. Queen Victoria [72]
29. Charles Darwin [72-73]
30. Mustafa Kemal Atatürk [82]
31. Nicholas II [86]
32. Grigori Rasputin [86]
33. Vladimir Lenin [86-87]
34. Joseph Stalin [87]
35. Benito Mussolini [92]
36. Adolf Hitler [93]
37. Friedrich Nietzsche [93]
38. Joseph Goebbels [93]
39. Francisco Franco [93]
40. Elie Wiesel [98]
41. Anne Frank [98]
42. Lech Walesa [106]
43. Ho Chi Minh [106]
44. Pol Pot [107]
45. Aung San Suu Kyi [107-108]
46. Sun Yixian [112]
47. Mao Zedong [112-114]
48. Mohandas Gandhi [115]
49. Benazir Bhutto [116]
50. Golda Meir [120]
51. Nelson Mandela [122]
52. Jomo Kenyatta [122]

Religion and Philosophy...What You Need to Know

1. Animism [5]
2. Shintoism [5]
3. Hinduism [5]
4. Buddhism [5-6]
5. Jainism [6]
6. Confucianism [6]

7. Daoism [6]
8. Islam [6-7]
9. Judaism [7]
10. Christianity [7-8]
11. Zoroastrianism [13]

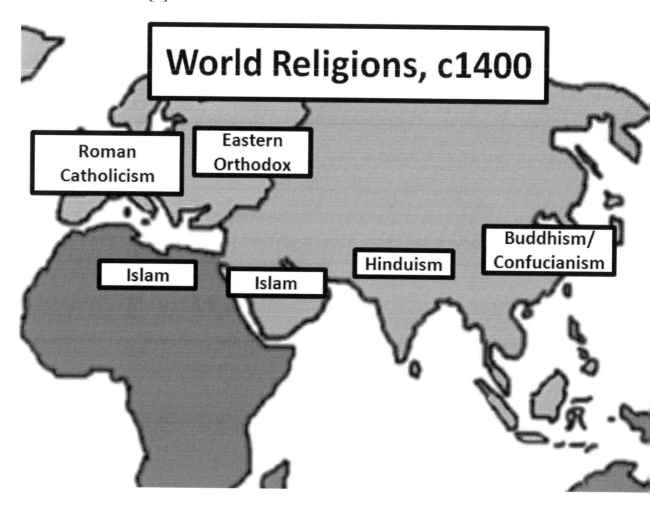

World Religions, c1400

Roman Catholicism

Eastern Orthodox

Islam

Islam

Hinduism

Buddhism/ Confucianism

ost Important Empires to Know (Pre-1820)

. Han Dynasty [20]

. Tang and Song Dynasties [21]

. Mongol Empire [21-22]

. Khmer Empire [22]

. Mauryan and Gupta Empires [23]

. Mughal Empire [23]

. Umayyads and Abbasid Empire [23-24]

. Ottoman Empire [25]

. Safavid Empire [25]

. Empire of Alexander the Great and Hel-

lenistic Culture [30-31]

11. Roman Empire before Caesar [31]

12. Byzantine Empire [32-33]

13. Carolingian Empire and Charlemagne [37]

14. Ghana, Mali, and Songhai Empires of Africa [47-48]

15. Mayan Empire [48-49]

16. Aztec Empire [49]

17. Incan Empire [49]

18. Napoleonic Empire [66]

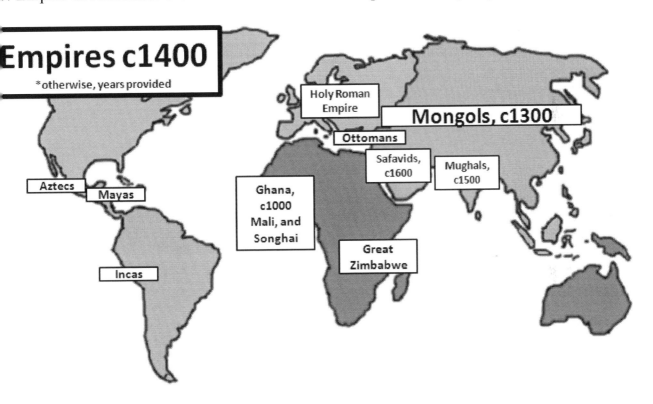

Wars and Conflict

1. Peloponnesian War [29]
2. Punic Wars [31]
3. The Crusades [38-39]
4. Hundred Years' War [40]
5. Thirty Years' War [56]
6. English Civil War [57]
7. Glorious Revolution [57]
8. French Revolution [63-65]
9. Napoleon's Invasion of Russia [66]
10. Unification of Italy [70]
11. Unification of Germany [70]
12. Boer Wars [77]
13. Crimean War [77-78]
14. Opium Wars [78]
15. Sepoy Rebellion [78]
16. Boxer Rebellion [79]
17. Russo-Japanese War [80]
18. World War I [80-81]
19. Bolshevik Revolution [87]
20. Russian Civil War [87]
21. World War II [94-96]
22. Cold War [102]
23. Soviet-Afghanistan War [104]
24. Korean War [106]
25. Vietnam War [106-107]
26. Chinese Civil War [113]
27. Iranian Revolution [121]

Twentieth Century Human Rights Violations

1. Armenian Massacres [82]
2. Pogroms [86]
3. Russia's Bloody Sunday [86]
4. Great Purge [88]
5. Nanjing Massacre [94]
6. Final Solution (Holocaust) [97-98]
7. Ethnic Cleansing in Bosnia [106]
8. Khmer Rouge [107]
9. Cultural Revolution [114]
10. Tiananmen Square Massacre [114]
11. Amritsar Massacre [115]
12. Apartheid [122]
13. Rwandan Genocide [122]
14. War in Darfur [122-123]

eography

1. Why did civilizations develop near water? [12]

2. Why was Mesopotamia called the Fertile Crescent? [12]

3. What rivers of China should I know? [19]

4. What impact did being a group of islands have on Japan? [22]

5. What are the important aspects of Indian geography? [22-23]

6. How did Greece's geography affect its development [29]

7. How diverse is Africa's climate? [47]

8. What is a physical map? [49]

9. Why couldn't Napoleon defeat Britain? [66]

0. Why did the Industrial Revolution begin in England? [71]

1. What does the Suez Canal connect? [120]

2. What are some of the environmental problems plaguing the Earth today? [123-124]

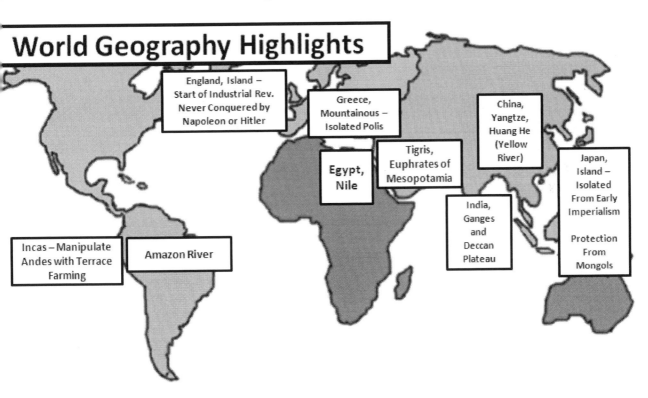

Women's Rights

Increased:

1. Hatshepsut [15]
2. Wu Zhao [21]
3. Justinian's Code [32-33]
4. Peter the Great [56]
5. Mary Wollstonecraft [58]
6. Mustafa Kemal Atatürk [82]
7. Soviet Union [87]
8. Mao in China [113]
9. Benazir Bhutto [116]
10. Aung San Suu Kyi [107-108]

Decreased:

1. Hammurabi's Code [13]
2. Ancient China [21]
3. Athenian Democracy [29]
4. Fate of Olympe de Gouges [65]
5. Napoleonic Code [66]

Examples of Cultural Diffusion

1. Definition of Cultural Diffusion [12-13]
2. Phoenician Alphabet [13]
3. Silk Roads [23]
4. Muslim and Greco-Roman Architecture [24-25]
5. Hellenistic Culture [30-31]
6. Greco-Roman/Western Civilization [32]
7. Cyrillic Alphabet [33]
8. Hanseatic League [38]
9. Results of the Crusades [39]
10. Mansa Musa [48]
11. Columbian Exchange [51]
12. Mestizo Culture [52]
13. Westernization of Russia [56]
14. Enlightenment in Latin America [67]
15. Industrial Revolution [70]
16. Meiji Era [79-80]
17. Global Interdependence [123]

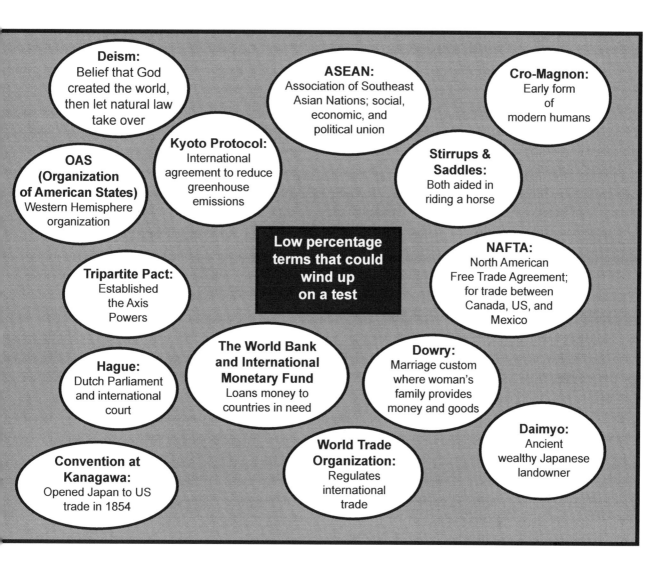

Low percentage terms that could wind up on a test

Deism: Belief that God created the world, then let natural law take over

ASEAN: Association of Southeast Asian Nations; social, economic, and political union

Cro-Magnon: Early form of modern humans

Kyoto Protocol: International agreement to reduce greenhouse emissions

OAS (Organization of American States) Western Hemisphere organization

Stirrups & Saddles: Both aided in riding a horse

Tripartite Pact: Established the Axis Powers

NAFTA: North American Free Trade Agreement; for trade between Canada, US, and Mexico

Hague: Dutch Parliament and international court

The World Bank and International Monetary Fund Loans money to countries in need

Dowry: Marriage custom where woman's family provides money and goods

Daimyo: Ancient wealthy Japanese landowner

Convention at Kanagawa: Opened Japan to US trade in 1854

World Trade Organization: Regulates international trade

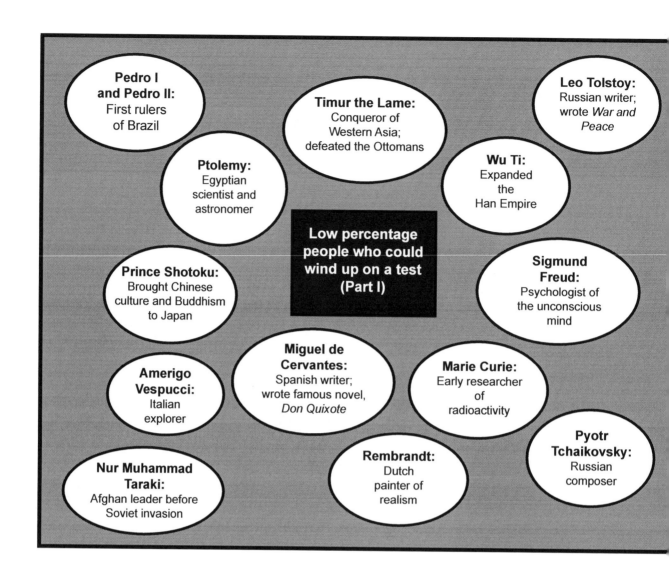

Low percentage people who could wind up on a test (Part I)

Pedro I and Pedro II: First rulers of Brazil

Timur the Lame: Conqueror of Western Asia; defeated the Ottomans

Leo Tolstoy: Russian writer; wrote *War and Peace*

Ptolemy: Egyptian scientist and astronomer

Wu Ti: Expanded the Han Empire

Prince Shotoku: Brought Chinese culture and Buddhism to Japan

Sigmund Freud: Psychologist of the unconscious mind

Amerigo Vespucci: Italian explorer

Miguel de Cervantes: Spanish writer; wrote famous novel, *Don Quixote*

Marie Curie: Early researcher of radioactivity

Pyotr Tchaikovsky: Russian composer

Nur Muhammad Taraki: Afghan leader before Soviet invasion

Rembrandt: Dutch painter of realism